# Mayo Clinic on Depression

**Keith Kramlinger, M.D.**

Editor-in-Chief

**MASON CREST PUBLISHERS**

Philadelphia, Pennsylvania

*Mayo Clinic on Depression* provides reliable, practical, easy-to-understand information on recognizing, treating and managing depression. Much of this information comes directly from the experience of phychiatrists, psychologists and other health care professionals at Mayo Clinic. This book supplements the advice of your physician, whom you should consult for individual medical problems. *Mayo Clinic on Depression* does not endorse any company or product. MAYO, MAYO CLINIC, MAYO CLINIC HEALTH INFORMATION and the Mayo triple-shield logo are marks of Mayo Foundation for Medical Education and Research.

Hardcover Library Edition Published 2002
Mason Crest Publishers
370 Reed Road
Suite 302
Broomall, PA  19008-0914
(866) MCP-BOOK (toll free)

First printing

1 2 3 4 5 6 7 8 9 10

Library of Congress Cataloging-in-Publication Data on file at the Library of Congress

ISBN 1-59084-226-X

Photo credits: Cover photos and the photos on pages 1, 59, 127 and 163 are from PhotoDisc.

Printed in the United States of America

## About depression

Depression affects an estimated 18 million Americans each year — more people than cancer and almost as many people as heart disease. But unlike cancer or heart disease, many people don't know what depression is or how to deal with it.

Depression is more than having a bad day, feeling sad for a brief period or grieving a loss in your life. It's an illness that affects how you think, feel and act. Depression may result from a complex interplay of factors that can trigger changes in brain activity. Contrary to long-held beliefs, depression isn't the result of personal weakness, and you simply can't "get over" depression or "snap out of it."

With proper treatment nearly 80 percent of people experiencing depression improve. But the process can take time. Within these pages, you'll find information to help you better understand depression and its treatment, and what you can do to help manage the illness. This book is based on the expertise of Mayo Clinic health care professionals and the advice they give day in and day out.

## About Mayo Clinic

Mayo Clinic evolved from the frontier practice of Dr. William Worrall Mayo and the partnership of his two sons, William J. and Charles H. Mayo, in the early 1900s. Pressed by the demands of their busy practice in Rochester, Minn., the Mayo brothers invited other physicians to join them, pioneering the private group practice of medicine. Today, with more than 2,000 physicians and scientists at its three major locations in Rochester, Minn., Jacksonville, Fla., and Scottsdale, Ariz., Mayo Clinic is dedicated to providing comprehensive diagnoses, accurate answers and effective treatments.

With this depth of medical knowledge, experience and expertise, Mayo Clinic occupies an unparalleled position as a health information resource. Since 1983, Mayo Clinic has published reliable health information for millions of consumers through award-winning newsletters, books and online services. Revenue from the publishing activities supports Mayo Clinic programs, including medical education and research.

## Editorial staff

**Editor in Chief**
Keith Kramlinger, M.D.

**Associate Medical Editors**
Matthew Clark, Ph.D.
Lois Krahn, M.D.
Kemuel Philbrick, M.D.
Richard Seime, Ph.D.
Bruce Sutor, M.D.
Lloyd Wells, M.D.

**Managing Editor**
Karen Wallevand

**Copy Editor**
Mary Duerson

**Proofreading**
Miranda Attlesey
Donna Hanson

**Editorial Research**
Deirdre Herman
Michelle Hewlett

**Contributing Writers**
Lee Engfer
Rebecca Gonzalez-Campoy
Tamara Kuhn
Stephen Miller
Carol Pearson, M.D.
Robin Silverman

**Creative Director**
Daniel Brevick

**Design**
Paul Krause

**Illustration and Photography**
Michael King
Richard Madsen
Christopher Srnka

**Indexing**
Larry Harrison

## Contributing editors and reviewers

Sara Berg, M.S.W.
Ann Decker, J.D.
Joanne Ericksen, R.N.
Christopher Frye
Mark Hansen, M.D.
Clifford Jack, M.D.
Siong-Chi Lin, M.D.

Toshihiko Maruta, M.D.
Joseph Parisi, M.D.
Keith Rasmussen, M.D.
Elliott Richelson, M.D.
Christine Sadowski, Ph.D.
Shirlene Sampson, M.D.

# Preface

You may have picked up this book because you're depressed, or you think that you may be, and you want to know how you can feel better again. Maybe you've experienced depression in the past, and you're searching for solutions to keep it from coming back. Or perhaps you have a close family member or friend with depression, and you're looking for ways that you can be of help. These are all common worries and concerns — and good reasons to read this book.

Nearly everyone has feelings of sadness or despair at some point in their lives. It's when these feelings persist, recur or become severe that you may be experiencing depression and should seek medical help. Depression is a common illness and one that can often be successfully treated. Unfortunately, too many people don't seek treatment for depression, either because they're unaware that they're depressed or because of misconceptions that depression isn't a real illness ("all in your head") and occurs only in people who are mentally weak.

Today, more than ever, doctors are aware of what it takes to treat depression to help you live a healthy and productive life. In this book, you'll find practical and easy-to-read information to help you understand depression. We begin with an explanation of the illness, who's at risk and what's known about its biology. We describe how to recognize and get help for depression, and we explain its several types. We then provide a comprehensive overview of the various treatments for depression, including self-help measures to manage or prevent it. Finally, we provide information specifically for special groups, including women, older adults, youth, and family and friends of depressed individuals.

Along with the advice of your doctor, this book can help you feel assured you're doing the right things to overcome depression so that you can return to a full and active life.

*Keith Kramlinger, M.D.*
Editor in Chief

# Contents

*Preface*                                                                    v

# Part 1: **Understanding Depression**

*Chapter 1*  **What is depression?**                                         3
    Defining depression                                  4
    A medical disorder                                   5
    Who gets depressed?                                  7
    How common is depression?                           7
    How it feels to be depressed                        9
    Voices of experience                                10
    An underrecognized illness                          12
    The importance of treatment                         13

*Chapter 2*  **Are you at risk?**                                            17
    Family history                                       17
    Genetics                                             18
    Stressful situations                                 18
    Past experiences                                     20
    Chemical dependence                                  23
    Prescription medications                             23
    Medical conditions                                   24
    Psychological issues                                 27
    Other mental illnesses                               28

*Chapter 3*  **The biology of depression**                                   31
    Family, adoption and twin studies                    31
    Hormone studies                                      33
    Brain imaging studies                                35
    Medication studies                                   37
    *Color section*                                      C1

| | | |
|---|---|---|
| *Chapter 4* | **Recognizing and diagnosing depression** | 39 |
| | What are the warning signs? | 39 |
| | Pathways for getting help | 42 |
| | Who provides mental health care? | 42 |
| | Where to start? | 45 |
| | Steps to diagnosis | 45 |
| | | |
| *Chapter 5* | **Types of depression** | 49 |
| | Major depression | 49 |
| | Dysthymia | 50 |
| | Adjustment disorders | 51 |
| | Bipolar disorders | 52 |
| | Other dimensions of depression | 55 |
| | Additional terms | 57 |
| | Getting it right | 58 |

# Part 2: Treating Depression

| | | |
|---|---|---|
| *Chapter 6* | **A treatment overview** | 61 |
| | A century of progress | 61 |
| | One treatment doesn't fit all | 65 |
| | | |
| *Chapter 7* | **Medications and how they work** | 67 |
| | Types of antidepressants | 67 |
| | Serotonin reuptake inhibitors | 69 |
| | Mixed reuptake inhibitors | 70 |
| | Receptor blockers | 71 |
| | Reuptake inhibitors and receptor blockers | 71 |
| | Enzyme inhibitors | 72 |
| | Choosing an antidepressant | 73 |
| | Additional medications | 76 |
| | New medications under study | 80 |
| | Herbal and dietary supplements | 81 |
| | | |
| *Chapter 8* | **Counseling and psychotherapy** | 85 |
| | Counseling | 85 |
| | Psychotherapy | 87 |

Cognitive behavior therapy ........................................... 88
Interpersonal therapy ................................................... 91
Other forms of psychotherapy ..................................... 92
How long does psychotherapy last? .............................. 93
How does psychotherapy work? .................................... 94
Making it work ........................................................... 96

*Chapter 9* **Electroconvulsive and other biomedical therapies** 97
Electroconvulsive therapy ........................................... 97
Light therapy ........................................................... 105
Possible future therapies: TMS and VNS ..................... 108

*Chapter 10* **Self-help strategies** .................................... 111
Getting through the rough times ................................. 111
Prescription for healthy living ..................................... 112
Caring for your physical health ................................... 113
Boosting your emotional health .................................. 119
Attending to your spiritual needs ................................ 125
The best defense is a good offense ............................. 126

# Part 3: Special Groups and Concerns

*Chapter 11* **Women and depression** ................................ 129
Why are women more vulnerable? .............................. 129
Depression during the reproductive years .................... 130
Premenstrual dysphoric disorder ................................ 130
Depression during pregnancy ..................................... 131
Postpartum depression .............................................. 132
Menopause and depression ....................................... 133
Social and cultural issues .......................................... 135
With help comes hope ............................................... 137

*Chapter 12* **Older adults and depression** ....................... 139
Common triggers ...................................................... 139
Recognizing depression in older adults ....................... 140
Alzheimer's, Parkinson's and depression ..................... 141
Stroke and depression .............................................. 143

Treating depression in older adults                                       143

Managing depression                                                       144

*Chapter 13* **Childhood and teenage depression**                         145

What to watch for                                                         146

Is your child at risk?                                                    147

Related conditions                                                        148

Treating depression in youth                                             151

Greater emphasis on early intervention                                    154

*Chapter 14* **Combined disorders**                                       155

Anxiety and depression                                                    156

Substance abuse and depression                                            157

Eating disorders and depression                                           158

Body dysmorphic disorder and depression                                   160

Personality disorders and depression                                      160

Telling it like it is                                                     162

# Part 4: Living With a Depressed Person

*Chapter 15* **Suicide and coping with suicide**                          165

Who's at risk?                                                            165

Warning signs                                                             167

Dealing with suicidal thoughts and actions                                168

Suicide survivors: Those left behind                                      169

*Chapter 16* **The role of family and friends**                           173

Being there                                                               173

Dealing with resistance                                                   175

Bearing the burden                                                        175

Taking care of yourself                                                   177

A balancing act                                                           178

*Facing and overcoming depression: A personal story*                      179

*Additional resources*                                                    185

*Index*                                                                   187

# Part 1

*Understanding Depression*

# Chapter 1

# *What is depression?*

Depression, wrote the novelist William Styron, is a "true
wimp of a word for such a major illness." The bland term
didn't reflect the anguish he'd known when depressed.

The word *depression* has many meanings. It's a common term for
a rut or a hollow in the ground. In the financial world, it means a
period of economic decline. In meteorology, it refers to a tropical
weather pattern that can spawn a cyclone or a hurricane. Among
astronomers, depression is the distance of a celestial object below
the horizon. But perhaps the most familiar meaning of the word
relates to mood. In casual usage, depression describes a temporary
low mood that may come from a bad day or a bad feeling. In medical terms, depression is a serious illness that causes memory and
thinking (cognitive), mood, physical and behavioral changes. It
affects how you feel, think, eat, sleep and act.

Many people — both those who've experienced the illness and
family and friends who've helped loved ones cope with it — are
familiar with the far-reaching effects of depression. Depression is
one of the most common medical problems in the United States and
around the world. At some point in their life, about one in four
Americans will experience at least one episode of depression.

The good news is that depression is treatable. Thanks to
improved medications and the availability of other medical and
psychological therapies, you can overcome depression, not just

endure it. With proper treatment, most people with depression improve — typically within weeks — and return to their usual activities. Their energy and zest for life gradually return, and brightness comes back to what seemed a dreary and dark world.

This book can help you better understand why depression occurs, how it can affect your life and what you can do to overcome this complex, often troubling and potentially serious illness. In it you'll also find information for specific groups, including women, children and older adults, and for people with specific concerns and circumstances, for example, those whose depression is associated with another mental illness.

## Defining depression

Depression has always existed. Descriptions of depressive maladies can be found in the texts of many ancient civilizations. In the Old Testament, King Saul, exhibiting classic signs of depression, is troubled by an "evil spirit" and eventually commits suicide. Early English texts refer to *melancholia,* which for centuries was the word used to describe mood disorders. The English writers Chaucer and Shakespeare both wrote about melancholy.

The earliest medical descriptions of depression date back to Hippocrates, the Greek "father of medicine" who lived in the fourth century B.C. Hippocrates believed mental illness resulted from natural causes rather than supernatural forces. He theorized that melancholia was a byproduct of excess black bile in the spleen — hence *melan* for "black" and *cholia* for "bile." To overcome depression, Hippocrates recommended a rebalancing of body systems using relaxation and healthy living strategies — components of which are still used as part of an overall treatment approach.

Over the centuries, other philosophers and physicians have attempted to define and understand depression. Just as the word *depression* in its common usage is vague, with different meanings, the illness itself isn't always easy to define or recognize. Its symptoms may overlap with symptoms of other illnesses, or they may be attributed to grief, stress, sleep problems, aging or overwork.

Many people say they're depressed when they feel sad, lonely, down or dejected: "I'm so depressed. I have so much work to do. I'm afraid I'll never get it all done!" But the medical illness of depression is more than a fleeting bad mood or period of stress. True depression — what doctors often refer to as depressive illness or clinical depression — is different from normal sadness or despair. Depressive illness, in its most common form, is characterized by the following:

- Lasts at least 2 weeks, often much longer
- Exhibits specific symptoms related to mood, behavior, thinking and outlook
- Impairs your ability to function on a daily basis
- Requires medical or psychological treatment or both

In this book, when we use the word *depression*, we're referring to the medical illness of depression.

## A medical disorder

For centuries, people viewed depression as a sign of physical or mental weakness and often rejected it as a legitimate health problem. "It's all in your head," was a common phrase heard by people experiencing depression. Following years of research, doctors now recognize depression as a medical disorder — an illness with a biological basis that's often influenced by psychological and social stress. A complex interplay of factors involving genetics, stress, and changes in body and brain function are thought to play a role in the development of depression. People with depression may have abnormally low levels of certain brain chemicals and slowed cellular activity in areas of the brain that control mood, appetite, sleep and other functions.

Depression can affect more than just your mood. It can also disrupt your sleeping and eating patterns and reduce your sexual drive. It filters how you think about things, making your thoughts more negative and pessimistic. It affects how you feel about yourself, lowering your sense of self-worth. It impacts how you act, often making you more irritable and ambivalent.

Depression can occur by itself, or it can be a complication of another illness. It may occur as a reaction to a medication or a drug. It may occur after childbirth or as a result of alcohol or drug abuse. It can be a response to stress from a job change, loss of a loved one or another difficult event. Sometimes it just happens, with no apparent trigger.

## Beyond the blues

Everyone experiences moments of unhappiness, often in response to a loss, a setback or the simple hassles of day-to-day living. The feelings that go along with these events are usually unpleasant, but temporary.

Occasional sadness that everyone feels because of life's disappointments is very different from depression. Depression is more than a passing bad mood or a case of the blues, a period of several days when you seem to be in a funk. Depression also isn't the same as having a bad attitude or being pessimistic.

In contrast to the blues or pessimism, depression continues for a longer period of time. Feelings of sadness or being down in the dumps persist and are often accompanied by other emotions, such as anxiety, anger, irritability, guilt or feelings of hopelessness. Unlike the blues or being pessimistic, depression can be debilitating.

## Greater than grief

Grief is a normal and necessary response to a significant loss, such as the death of a loved one, the end of a relationship, a move to a new town, a change in your health or the death of a pet. In many ways, grief and depression are similar. Symptoms common to both are feelings of sadness, lack of interest in usually pleasurable activities, and problems with sleeping and eating. Although grief is a normal and healthy process, depression is not.

The differences between grief and depression are in how long the feelings last and to what extent your daily activities are impaired. Depression can complicate grief in two ways: It can produce short-term symptoms that are more severe than those normally associated with grief. And it can cause symptoms of grief to persist longer than normal and possibly worsen. Grief generally lasts up to a year. If your grief is severe or lasts longer, it may be complicated by depression. Studies attempting to clarify key differences between grief and depression suggest that one difference between the two is self-denigration: People who are depressed often have feelings of worthlessness. People who are grieving generally don't.

## Who gets depressed?

Depression can strike anyone, regardless of age, race, nationality, occupation, income level or sex. Women, though, have significantly higher rates of depression than men do. This difference may be due in part to biological causes. Past life experiences, including sexual and domestic abuse, also may play a role. Abuse isn't exclusive to women, but it does occur more frequently among women than among men.

A person's first episode of depression typically occurs in the prime of life, between the ages of 25 and 44. However, the illness also affects children, teenagers and older adults.

Depression rates are lower among married people and those in long-term, intimate relationships. The disease is significantly more common among people who are divorced or separated. Although it's uncertain why, depression also seems to be more prominent among highly creative individuals (see "An Accomplished Group" on the following page).

## How common is depression?

If you're depressed, you're not alone. Depression is one of the most common medical problems in the United States. It affects approximately 18 million American adults at any given time. At some point in their life, close to one-fourth of all Americans will experience at least one episode of depression. However, many people don't recognize their illness, and some doctors are reluctant to diagnose it.

In a recent survey, 7 percent of U.S. adults said they have experienced a mental health problem, and 26 percent said they have felt

## An accomplished group

"The mind is its own place, and of itself / Can make a Heaven of Hell, a Hell of Heaven," wrote the 17th-century poet John Milton in his masterpiece *Paradise Lost*. Two centuries later, another poet who knew something about mood swings, Lord Byron, described "the apostle of affliction" who "from woe wrung overwhelming eloquence."

The list of creative talents who have experienced depression is long and impressive. It includes musicians Robert Schumann, Ludwig van Beethoven, Peter Tchaikovsky, and John Lennon, artists Vincent van Gogh and Georgia O'Keeffe, and writers Edgar Allan Poe, Mark Twain, Virginia Woolf, Ernest Hemingway, F. Scott Fitzgerald, and Sylvia Plath.

Speculation about a connection between creativity and depression dates back to the ancient Greeks. They believed that divine forms of madness inspired mortals' creative acts. Modern scientists have conducted dozens of studies exploring this link. Although the evidence is sketchy, some researchers have found that depression tends to be more common among poets, writers, artists and composers. In one study, this group experienced twice the rate of serious depression than that of people in other fields.

Other researchers caution that the link between creativity and depression is exaggerated and that plenty of creative people are emotionally stable. Most investigators believe that creative achievement occurs despite, not because of, emotional illness. Depression can just as easily stifle creativity as enhance it.

close to a nervous breakdown. The term *nervous breakdown* isn't an official medical or scientific term, but findings from this study provide additional support for how commonly people experience symptoms of mental illness.

Depression isn't just a phenomenon in the United States. On a worldwide basis, depression ranks fourth as a cause of disability and early death, according to the Global Burden of Disease Study conducted by the Harvard School of Public Health, the World Health Organization (WHO) and the World Bank. There's also evidence that depression is becoming more prevalent. Several studies suggest slightly increasing rates of depression over time — although it's uncertain whether the higher rates stem from an actual increase in the illness or increased reporting of depression. Authors of the Global Burden of Disease Study predict that in the year 2020, depression could become the second most serious health threat worldwide, behind only heart disease.

## How it feels to be depressed

Depression often presents itself in four major ways. It's not uncommon for people who know you well to notice these changes before you do. (Signs and symptoms of depression are discussed in greater detail in Chapter 4.)

### Mood changes

A hallmark symptom of depression is a depressed mood. You may feel sad, helpless, and hopeless and find yourself having crying spells. It's also common for your self-esteem and self-confidence to plummet during periods of depression. Many people with depression feel guilty or worthless.

Not all people with depression, however, feel depressed. Other emotions may be more pronounced. You might feel agitated. You may find yourself increasingly irritable and easily annoyed. Or you might become bored and find that nothing seems exciting to you anymore. Usually enjoyable activities no longer bring you pleasure or hold your interest.

### Cognitive changes

Depression can interfere with your memory and thought process. You may have trouble concentrating. You may find that you struggle whenever you have to make a decision. Even relatively simple decisions, such as deciding what clothes to wear or meals to prepare, can seem complicated and time consuming. As a result, you may find it more difficult to get things done.

### Physical changes

Depression can affect many areas of physical functioning. For example, it can wreak havoc on your sleeping and eating habits. You may wake up at 4 or 5 a.m. and not be able to get back to sleep, or you may feel like sleeping all day and spend too many hours in bed. You might overeat and gain weight, or lose your appetite and lose weight. Your sex drive may diminish or disappear.

Depression can sap your energy. People with depression often feel tired, slowed down or burned out. Getting out of bed in the morning or preparing and eating a meal can feel like a monumental effort. Depression is also linked to a variety of vague physical complaints, such as headache, backache, abdominal pain, and aches and pains without an obvious medical explanation.

### Behavior changes

Depression may change behavior in many ways. If you're normally well-groomed, you might start neglecting your appearance. If you've always been careful about paying bills, you may lose track of them. You may withdraw from people, preferring to stay home. Conflicts might become more frequent with your spouse or other family members. At work, you might fall behind on deadlines.

## Voices of experience

Here's how some people who've lived with depression describe their experience.

*During the worst periods, my depression is the classic 'black cloud' over the head — a 'black clamp' is more accurate. It feels as though something is actually pressing on my head — something incredibly oppressive. During these periods, it is hard to recall ever not being depressed. The depression seems to consume me for the past and future. I have also experienced more mild depressions, which just sapped my energy and optimism but didn't feel as devastating.*
Margaret
Santa Fe, New Mexico

## A voice from the past

*I am now the most miserable man living. If what I feel were equally distributed to the whole human family, there would be not one cheerful face on earth. Whether I shall ever be better, I cannot tell. I awfully forebode I shall not. To remain as I am is impossible. I must die or be better it appears to me.*

Abraham Lincoln, the future 16th president of the United States, wrote these words to a close friend in 1841.

*I feel like I'm in a cardboard box and the lid is too low. I have to expend a huge amount of energy trying to do what I'd easily do when not depressed. Also, I'll have days where the depression feels like a chemical mix-up — I feel normal then it switches, and I feel low and unable to function, and nothing I can pinpoint has changed.*

Cathy
Minneapolis

*I feel flat, helpless. Often panicky, trapped, hopeless. Sometimes crying and great sadness, other times just numb. Feelings of worthlessness are common.*

Anne
Los Angeles

*When depressed, I feel dark, numb, scared, naturally self-blaming, seemingly unable to move, both literally and figuratively — with a hopeless feeling. Other feelings — cynical, empty inside and worthless.*

Larry
Englewood, New Jersey

*Depression has affected many of my friendships by sapping the energy needed to be a good friend and maintain friendships, and by causing me to withdraw from friends. It's also affected romantic relationships in a similar way. I wouldn't say that it's caused the breakup of any romantic relationships, but it's been a contributing factor once or twice.*

Amy
Kansas City, Missouri

*Inability to concentrate is definitely a symptom of depression for me. I have trouble finishing projects or putting my best foot forward on a creative project. Lack of appetite is never a problem. In fact, depression makes me only want to eat more. One winter a few years ago, when depressed, I consumed a pint of Ben & Jerry's every night, and proceeded to gain 20 pounds. The weight stayed with me, too, and has been hard to shake off, like depression itself.*

Elizabeth
Eugene, Oregon

## An underrecognized illness

Although depression is common, about one-third of people with depression don't know they have it. And of those who do, two-thirds don't get proper treatment. Reasons why include:

**Limited recognition.** Some people don't recognize their depressive symptoms and the need for treatment. Many think the troubles they're having are a normal part of life. This is especially true if the prominent mood symptoms are agitation, irritation, anxiety or loss of pleasure in usual activities, rather than a depressed mood.

Sometimes not all of the signs and symptoms of depression are present, or they show up with different levels of intensity. For example, your biggest symptom could be sleeplessness, and you might not notice any other signs. Likewise, your doctor may not see the full picture if, for instance, your main concern is fatigue. Unfortunately, studies show that doctors commonly fail to diagnose depression.

**Embarrassment and confidentiality.** Some people are embarrassed to seek help because they fear that depression carries a stigma: "Will my family or friends think I'm weak, or not understand?" Concerns about employer confidentiality also prevent some people from seeking treatment: "I've heard my supervisor say that she thought a co-worker with depression was 'faking it' and 'just trying to get out of work.' Will she think the same thing about me?"

**Insurance concerns.** Some people worry that they'll have trouble getting or keeping insurance coverage if they receive a diagnosis of depression. Some health plans don't cover treatment for depression. Fortunately, these concerns are less of a reality than they were several years ago, but there's still need for improvement.

**Effects of the illness.** The feelings of hopelessness and helplessness brought on by depression can make it difficult to take the necessary steps to get treatment.

## The importance of treatment

Depression is treatable, and often with good results. With appropriate treatment, approximately 8 out of 10 people with depression will improve and can return to their usual, productive lives.

Once you suspect or recognize depression, it's crucial that you take steps to treat the illness. Untreated depression can raise your risk of a number of other health conditions. Studies show that even mild depression may be associated with poor physical and social functioning, increased risk of future depression and suicide attempts. Treating depression brings many benefits.

### Better quality of life

Most people who receive treatment for depression experience noticeable changes in two important areas: their personal relationships and their performance of daily work.

**Personal relationships.** When you're depressed, problems with people who are close to you may develop or worsen. Depression puts tremendous stress on a marriage or other personal relationships. You may say and do hurtful things, such as lashing out at your partner or saying that you hate everything in your life or that you're miserable in your marriage or relationship. Some people who blame their marriage or relationship for their unhappiness are depressed. After their depression is treated, they often feel more hopeful and positive and can more effectively work on a marriage or another relationship that needs help.

Your depression can also have a significant effect on your children. Focused on your own suffering or immobilized by your illness, you may not be able to respond to your children's needs.

Depression makes it harder to be active, so you might stop playing with the kids or doing activities you used to enjoy together.

**Work performance.** Depression can interfere with your ability to concentrate and remember, affecting your ability to do your daily work. Or you may have trouble getting out of bed and making it to work or school on time. Treating depression can reduce pressure at work by improving your concentration level and helping you sleep better so that you have more energy in the morning.

### Avoidance of addictions
Untreated depression can lead to other problems, including addiction. Studies demonstrate that some people with serious depression are at increased risk of substance abuse. Using alcohol and other drugs to "drown their sorrows" is one way some people try to self-medicate their illness. But drinking alcohol or taking drugs to ease the pain of depression leads to a vicious cycle because substance abuse can lead to or worsen depression.

### Improved health
Depression can have a wide range of physical effects. It can make existing medical conditions worse and may even increase the likelihood of getting some diseases. By treating depression, you'll not only feel better emotionally, but you'll be physically healthier.

Conditions associated with depression include:

**Insomnia.** Many people with depression have difficulty sleeping. They may have trouble falling asleep, they may wake up frequently during the night or they may awake in the early hours of the morning and be unable to go back to sleep. Treating depression can improve your sleep patterns and allow you to wake up feeling rested.

**Weight problems and lack of exercise.** Some people who are depressed overeat, resulting in significant weight gain. Being overweight is associated with many health risks, including increased risk of heart disease, high blood pressure and diabetes. Other people experiencing depression lose their appetite, lose weight and can become dangerously thin.

People who experience the lack of energy and motivation associated with depression commonly get little exercise and are physically unfit. Even people who were formerly very active may stop exercising. Treating depression — especially when combined with exercise and a healthy diet — can reduce risks associated with poor fitness and an unhealthy weight.

**Heart disease and stroke.** People who are depressed have a greater risk of heart attack, heart failure and stroke. Men who are depressed stand a greater chance of dying of heart disease.

As part of the large National Health and Nutrition Examination Survey, researchers studied 5,007 women and 2,886 men in the United States who were free of heart disease when they were interviewed. Eight to 10 years later, men in the group who were depressed were 2.7 times more likely to die of heart disease and 1.7 times more likely to die of any cause than men who weren't depressed. Depression didn't increase women's risk of dying of heart disease, but women who were depressed were almost twice as likely to develop heart disease.

In another study, researchers from the Cardiovascular Health Study Collaborative Research Group followed 4,493 people age 65 and older who were initially free of heart disease. After 6 years, those who most often reported symptoms of depression were 40 percent more likely to develop heart disease than were those who felt depressed the least often. Not all follow-up studies, however, found an association between depression and heart disease.

In yet another study, people who were depressed were more than four times more likely to have a heart attack in the next 13 years than were those who weren't depressed. Depression following a cardiac incident also brings an increased risk of complications or death.

Although more research is needed to understand the link between depression and heart disease, experts say there are plausible reasons for this mind-body connection. The bottom line is that treating depression may lessen your risk of having a heart attack or a stroke, or may reduce your risk of dying if you've recently had a heart attack.

**High blood pressure.** According to a study by the Centers for Disease Control and Prevention, depression is a risk factor for developing high blood pressure, a major cause of heart disease and stroke. People with the highest levels of depression and anxiety were at highest risk of developing high blood pressure. But even people with intermediate levels had a greater likelihood of developing high blood pressure. The risk is especially high for blacks.

**Other diseases.** Some research suggests a complex relationship between depression and conditions such as Parkinson's disease, Alzheimer's disease and osteoporosis (bone thinning) in women. It's not clear if depression itself makes a person more vulnerable to these diseases, nor is there a clear-cut cause-and-effect relationship. Research on these issues is still at an early stage.

### Reduced risk of recurrent episodes

Left untreated, depression may persist or worsen. In most instances it eventually goes away, but typically not until after months or years of distress and impairment.

Depression also can come back, and possibly be more severe. Your risk of having another bout of depression increases with each episode. If you've had one episode of depression, you stand a 50 percent chance of developing another. After two episodes, the risk goes up to 70 percent, and after three or more, it's even greater. Subsequent episodes often are longer, more severe and more difficult to treat. The sooner depression is recognized — whether it's a first or subsequent episode — often the easier it is to treat.

### Suicide prevention

A lag in diagnosis and treatment of depression can prove deadly. People with severe, untreated depression may have a suicide rate as high as 15 percent, compared with 1 percent in the general population. Untreated depression is the No. 1 cause of suicide in the United States. The risk of suicide increases with each episode of depression. With treatment, thoughts of suicide usually disappear.

## Chapter 2

# *Are you at risk?*

With any illness it's natural to wonder what causes it and if you're at risk. Like many other complex disorders, depression offers no simple answers. The illness may develop for a variety of reasons. That's why depression is so common.

The exact causes of depression are still being untangled, but scientists have identified a number of risk factors — events and conditions that increase your likelihood of becoming depressed. In many cases, depression results from not just one factor but a combination of them.

## Family history

If someone in your family has or had depression, that doesn't necessarily mean you'll develop it too. A family history of depression does, however, appear to increase your risk. This has been documented in numerous studies examining depression in families. The findings show that first degree relatives — parents, siblings, children — of a depressed person have a higher risk of depression than do individuals without a family history of depression. The increase in risk may be related to genetics, family environment or both.

Research also indicates that severe forms of depression and early-onset depression are more likely to run in families. Severe depression generally lasts a significant period of time, recurs several times and includes thoughts of death or suicide.

## Genetics

Genetic factors play a role in many human diseases. An inherited susceptibility to a disease occurs when a particular gene fails to give the correct instructions for cell functioning. This may make you more vulnerable to disease. Genes can also influence the severity or progression of a disease.

Although it's clear that a person can inherit a heightened risk of depression, the increase in risk doesn't appear to result from a single defective gene. More likely, it's linked to the interaction of multiple genes. In addition, genetic factors alone are probably not enough to trigger the illness — other factors also come into play. Researchers have found evidence of both genetic and nongenetic contributions to depression. Studies show that:

- Adopted children whose biological parents experienced depression are more likely to experience depression than adopted children without a family history of depression. This suggests a genetic link.
- Identical twins, who share the same genes, have a higher rate of both twins experiencing depression than do fraternal twins, who share only some of the same genes. This also suggests a genetic link.
- Among identical twins, when one twin becomes depressed, in only 40 percent of cases does the other twin experience depression. This indicates that other factors, such as stress or illness, also play a role. If genetics were solely responsible for depression, the occurrence would have been 100 percent.

## Stressful situations

No one gets through life without problems. Although life's losses and difficulties can spur personal or spiritual growth, they can also send you into a downward spiral. Stress runs the gamut from daily hassles, like traffic jams and financial worries, to major life events, such as the breakup of a significant relationship or a death in the family. Going through a stressful life event doesn't mean that you'll become depressed, but it can increase your risk.

### Death and other losses

A significant loss — even the threat of a loss — is one of the most common triggers of depression. Most people eventually move beyond the pain from grief and sadness, but others become depressed. The recent loss of a loved one is frequently associated with the development of depression. For a young child, death of a parent can be especially difficult to cope with. Other losses, such as a job layoff, also can lead to the illness. People who have experienced depression in the past are more vulnerable to depression following a significant loss.

### Relationship troubles

Troubles in a marriage or other intimate relationship can set off an episode of depression. In particular, divorce or the breakup of another significant relationship is a common precursor to depression. According to the Epidemiologic Catchment Area study — a comprehensive survey of 18,571 people in five U.S. cities — individuals who were divorced or separated were twice as likely as married people to experience a mental illness. Relationships don't prevent stress, but they do appear to serve as a buffer to the impact of life's upheavals.

### Major life events

Any big upheaval or life change can increase your risk of becoming depressed, especially if you have an inherited tendency toward depression. Life changes can range from surviving a catastrophe, like a serious automobile accident, to experiencing natural milestones, like puberty or retirement. Your general outlook on life influences how you handle these changes. Some people might see retirement as an ending and a loss, leading to symptoms of depression. Others might welcome retirement as a positive change.

### Putting the problem in perspective

Why do some people sink into depression because of major life troubles while others seemingly sail through them? There are many reasons for this, but one factor may be individual coping styles. An active, problem-solving style is less likely to result in depression than a passive, emotion-focused style. A positive coping style includes:

- Having a strong social and support network of friends and family
- Trying to take a positive view of the situation
- Using problem-solving skills to tackle the situation
- Discussing your problems and concerns with others and maintaining friendships

### Job stresses

Popular cartoons such as *Dilbert* attest to the commonplace and exasperating stresses of modern work life. In recent insurance industry studies, nearly half of American workers indicated their job is very or extremely stressful, and more than a quarter said their job was the greatest source of stress in their life. According to some studies, corporations lose about 16 days annually in productivity per worker due to stress, anxiety and depression.

Working mothers also face the stress of covering the "second shift" — often assuming primary responsibility for housework and child care. According to the Center for Research on Women at Wellesley College, having children gives working moms a mental and emotional boost, but it also increases their work and family strain — in turn increasing risk of depression.

## Past experiences

People who've survived deeply upsetting events in the past, such as childhood abuse, wartime combat or being a witness to a serious crime, are at higher risk of developing depression than are those who haven't had such experiences. Overwhelming stress can trigger a number of responses in the body with long-lasting effects on physical and mental health.

In a study of almost 10,000 adults, the more traumatic experiences a person had in childhood, the higher the individual's likelihood of developing depression. Several aspects of a troubled family environment may put children at risk of depression as an adult. These include:

- A high level of conflict between parents
- Family violence
- Abuse
- Loss of a parent due to separation, divorce or death
- Illness in a parent

Scientists have tried to explain the connection between past traumas and depression. It's partly related to the way the human body responds to danger and stress. When confronted with real or perceived danger, your body gears up to face the challenge ("fight") or musters enough strength to move out of trouble's way ("flight"). This fight-or-flight response results from the release of hormones that cause your body to shift into overdrive. These changes can influence brain activity, further alerting your brain to stress.

But hormones are only part of the equation. Your ability to cope with stress is another key factor. Children learn by example. If you're not taught good coping skills when growing up, you may be less able to cope with stress as an adult, and you may experience more stress than a person with better coping skills.

### Childhood abuse

Any form of abuse during childhood — sexual, physical or emotional — can make a person more vulnerable to depression. One study of almost 2,000 women revealed that those with a history of childhood sexual or physical abuse exhibited more signs and symptoms of depression and anxiety and attempted suicide more frequently than did women with no history of childhood abuse. Women who were abused as children are four times more likely to develop major depression in adulthood.

Childhood sexual abuse can be a devastating experience. An estimated 6 percent to 15 percent of women have experienced some form of sexual abuse during childhood. Childhood sexual abuse is less common among boys, but it does occur and is equally traumatic. A large number of studies have demonstrated a clear relationship between childhood sexual abuse and depression as an adult.

### Post-traumatic stress

It used to be called shell shock, or battle fatigue. Post-traumatic stress disorder (PTSD) is the modern name for this condition that can affect people who have lived through a horrific event. Besides military combat, other terrifying events that can trigger post-traumatic stress disorder include rape, torture, a severe automobile accident or a natural disaster.

People with post-traumatic stress disorder often experience flashbacks, nightmares, sleep problems, emotional numbness or sudden emotional outbursts, loss of pleasure, an exaggerated startle reflex, and problems with memory and concentration. They are also at increased risk of developing other mental illnesses, including depression. Post-traumatic stress disorder and depression often occur together.

### Growing up with an alcoholic

Some studies comparing adult children of alcoholics with adult children of nonalcoholics show that children of alcoholics are more likely to experience symptoms of anxiety and depression. But not all studies have found differences between the two groups.

The relationship between a parent's alcoholism and depression in his or her children appears complicated. It's difficult to separate the effects of parental alcoholism from other social and psychological factors, such as dysfunctional family relationships, a parent's depression or other mental illness, and trauma, abuse or neglect in childhood.

Studies of families have found high rates of depression among relatives of alcoholics. This could result from a higher prevalence of mood disorders in such families, or a genetic link between family alcoholism and depression. In addition, the stress of living in an alcoholic family may increase the risk of depression for reasons unrelated to genetics.

## Chemical dependence

Dependence on alcohol or drugs can increase your risk of depression. Thirty percent to 60 percent of people with substance abuse problems — alcohol, prescription medications or illegal drugs — also experience a mood or anxiety disorder. Approximately 20 percent of people who abuse drugs are depressed or have experienced depression in the past. Of people who abuse alcohol, about 30 percent meet the medical criteria for depression. When depression and chemical dependence occur simultaneously, they may be independent of each other, or one can be a result of the other.

Many researchers have questioned whether it's possible to inherit a tendency toward both alcoholism and depression. Researchers from the National Institute on Alcohol Abuse and Alcoholism analyzed survey data from 42,862 U.S. adults age 18 and older and found that a family history of alcoholism increased a person's likelihood of experiencing both alcoholism and depression. Both men and women with an alcoholic relative are more likely to develop depression than are those without an alcoholic relative. Women with an alcoholic relative are at slightly higher risk of depression than are men with an alcoholic relative. Researchers believe that the genetic factors that contribute to alcoholism and depression may overlap but aren't exactly the same.

## Prescription medications

Long-term use of some prescription medications may cause symptoms of depression in some people. These medications include:
- Corticosteroids, such as prednisone (Deltasone, Orasone)
- Interferon (Avonex, Rebetron), an anti-inflammatory drug
- Some bronchodilators used for asthma and other lung disorders, including theophylline (Slo-phyllin, Theo-Dur)
- Stimulants, including some diet pills, used long-term
- Sleeping pills and some anti-anxiety drugs (benzodiazepines), including diazepam (Valium) and chlordiazepoxide (Librium), used long-term

- Isotretinoin (Accutane), a medication used to treat acne
- Some blood pressure and heart medications, including the drug propranolol (Inderal)
- Oral contraceptives
- Anticancer drugs, such as tamoxifen (Nolvadex)

Sudden withdrawal from some medications, especially corticosteroids, also may lead to depression.

## Medical conditions

Many other illnesses and conditions can cause symptoms of depression, either directly or indirectly. Some hormonal diseases have a direct link to the development of depression. With other types of disease, the link is more roundabout. Arthritis, for example, may cause pain and interfere with your quality of life. These factors, in turn, can alter your mood and outlook, causing depression.

### Hormone-related diseases

Thyroid problems are commonly associated with depression. The thyroid gland produces and releases hormones that help regulate your body temperature, heart rate and metabolism, including how efficiently you burn calories. If the gland releases too much hormone (an overactive thyroid) your metabolism runs too fast. If it releases too little (an underactive thyroid) your metabolism slows.

Having an underactive thyroid (hypothyroidism) may cause depression. Many doctors routinely test levels of thyroid hormones before making a diagnosis of depression. If you have an underactive thyroid, your doctor will prescribe thyroid hormone medication to make up for the deficiency. This treatment usually brings an end to this type of depression.

Other conditions that stem from hormonal imbalances also can trigger depression. They include disorders of the parathyroid gland and of the adrenal glands (Cushing's and Addison's diseases).

### Heart disease

Just as being depressed increases your risk of developing heart disease or having a heart attack, the reverse also is true. Thirty percent of people who are hospitalized for coronary artery disease — obstruction in the arteries leading to the heart — experience some degree of depression. And up to half of people who've had a heart attack become depressed.

### Stroke

A stroke occurs when a blocked or ruptured blood vessel in your brain reduces your brain's blood supply. People who have had a stroke are at higher risk of developing depression. The illness is one of the most common complications of stroke, affecting up to 40 percent of people in the first 2 years following a stroke. Your degree of physical impairment following a stroke doesn't coincide with your risk of depression. People with mild impairment are at the same risk as those with more severe impairment.

It can be difficult to distinguish signs and symptoms of depression from the effects of stroke, which may include memory difficulties, agitation and fatigue. A prior history of depression may further increase your risk of becoming depressed after a stroke. Depression also increases the risk of death following a stroke.

### Cancer

Cancer commonly leads to depression. As many as one in five people with cancer become depressed. The rates are somewhat higher among people with advanced cancer. Among adults with cancer who are hospitalized, rates of depression range from 23 percent to 60 percent. People who have a history of depression are more likely to become depressed after getting cancer.

Depression often goes unrecognized and untreated among people with cancer for a couple of reasons. Sadness and grief are natural reactions to having cancer and can resemble depression. Signs and symptoms such as weight loss and fatigue also overlap. In addition, medical professionals and the general public are tempted to say, "I'd be depressed too if I had cancer," as if the fact that the association is understandable frees doctors and family or friends from doing anything about it. Consider this: If you came upon a man bleeding profusely after cutting himself with a chain saw would you say, "I'd be bleeding too if I cut myself with a chain saw," and then go on your way? More likely, your response would be to seek help for the man.

Treatment for depression has been shown to help improve mood, immune system functioning and quality of life in people with cancer.

### Alzheimer's disease

Depression is common among people with Alzheimer's disease, a progressive deterioration of the brain that causes memory loss and disorientation. Approximately 40 percent of people with Alzheimer's disease have depressed moods, and about 20 percent develop depression. Clues to the presence of depression in someone with Alzheimer's disease may include irritability, agitation and acting out. Treatment can lift the depression, but it won't stop the progression of Alzheimer's disease.

### Parkinson's disease

As with Alzheimer's disease, depression is a common companion to Parkinson's disease, which affects the nervous system and can result in tremors, rigid movement and a droopy posture. Forty percent to 50 percent of people with Parkinson's disease become depressed. Loss of appetite and sleep disturbances may be more severe in a person with both Parkinson's disease and depression.

A major international study, the Global Parkinson Disease Survey, examined factors that influence the quality of life for people with Parkinson's disease. The study found that the most troubling and disabling factor was depression, rather than the physical limitations caused by the disease or the effects of medications.

Researchers have noted that depression often precedes the development of Parkinson's disease and Alzheimer's disease, sometimes by more than a decade. They speculate that depression could be a risk factor for developing these diseases, but no definite link has been established.

### Obstructive sleep apnea

Obstructive sleep apnea is characterized by severe snoring and irregular breathing patterns while you sleep. Depression commonly accompanies obstructive sleep apnea and can improve dramatically with proper treatment of the sleep disorder.

### Chronic pain

Chronic pain and depression often go hand in hand. Persistent pain combined with daily stress often creates an emotional sinkhole that can be difficult to escape. Studies indicate that up to half of people with chronic pain experience mild to severe depression.

### Other diseases and conditions

Other medical conditions that may increase the risk of depression include kidney disease, rheumatoid arthritis, chronic lung diseases, AIDS and human immunodeficiency virus (HIV) infection, a brain tumor or injury, a spinal cord injury, diabetes, multiple sclerosis, epilepsy and vitamin deficiencies.

## Psychological issues

Is the glass half full or half empty? How you answer that question might influence your risk of depression. Certain personality traits can make you more vulnerable to depression. You may be more prone to depression if you:
- Have low self-esteem
- Are overly self-critical
- Are habitually pessimistic
- Are easily overwhelmed by stress

### Optimists vs. pessimists

During the last 25 years, studies have shown that pessimistic people become depressed more easily than do optimists. Pessimists also have poorer health, use the health care system more often and may die sooner than optimists. A Mayo Clinic study published in February 2000 found that people who have optimistic outlooks generally live longer and healthier lives than their pessimistic counterparts. Mayo Clinic researchers surveyed a group of people who had taken a personality test 30 years before and compared each individual's test results with his or her present life and health status. They found that the survival rate among optimists was better than expected and that pessimists were at increased risk of early death.

Pessimists tend to interpret bad events differently than optimists do. They blame themselves and see events as permanent and pervasive: "This problem is going to last forever, and it's going to affect everything." In contrast, optimists often see bad events as specific, temporary and controllable.

### Learned helplessness

When people are in a difficult situation, such as an abusive relationship, they may come to believe that their efforts to control, change, predict or avoid the situation won't work, no matter what they do. As a result, they give up trying — they become helpless. This "learned helplessness" can develop into a common response to other facets of life, including work, family relationships and health problems. Experts believe that learned helplessness makes an individual more susceptible to depression.

## Other mental illnesses

Depression and other mental illnesses often go hand in hand. Doctors often refer to this as comorbid conditions.

### Anxiety disorders

Everyone worries on occasion. But worry can become overwhelming and interfere with your ability to enjoy and fully participate in life. Exaggerated or persistent worry is a symptom of anxiety disorder. Like depression, anxiety disorders are common, occurring in approximately 17 percent of the population.

Depression commonly accompanies anxiety. Up to 60 percent of people with an anxiety disorder also develop depression. Types of anxiety disorders include:

**Generalized anxiety disorder.** People with this disorder experience excessive anxiety and worry that's difficult to control. Their worries may also be accompanied by a fear that something bad is about to happen. Other symptoms may include restlessness, fatigue, difficulty concentrating and irritability.

**Social anxiety disorder.** People with social anxiety disorder, also called social phobia, are excessively afraid of social situations. They may be anxious when meeting strangers, talking on the telephone or attending parties. Or they may fear a particular situation, such as public speaking or being watched while eating. About one-third of people with social phobia are also depressed.

**Panic disorder.** The main features of panic disorder are panic attacks and the fear of an attack. During a panic attack, you feel a sudden, unexplainable terror. Physical signs and symptoms may include a pounding heart, sweating, trembling or shaking, difficulty breathing, chest pain, nausea, dizziness and tingling. You may believe that you're "going crazy" or that you're going to die.

More than one-third of Americans report having had a panic attack at some point in their life. People with panic disorder experience repeated panic attacks. Depression affects up to half of people with panic disorder.

**Obsessive-compulsive disorder.** Many people experience obsessive thoughts or compulsive behaviors at one time or another. Obsessions are intrusive, irrational thoughts that keep recurring. Compulsions are repetitive rituals such as checking that the doors are locked or the coffeepot is off. For people with obsessive-compulsive disorder (OCD), obsessive thoughts and compulsive behaviors take over their life, interfering with their ability to function.

The National Institute of Mental Health estimates that this disorder affects more than 2 percent of the U.S. population — between 4 million and 6 million people.

### Eating disorders

Depression is common among people with eating disorders. Individuals with an eating disorder may have a genetic susceptibility to the disorder, depression or both. Depression may contribute to an eating disorder, or it may result from one of the following disorders:

**Anorexia nervosa.** People with anorexia nervosa have an intense fear of becoming fat, and they may lose weight to the point of being malnourished. Not eating enough food deprives your body of energy and nutrients, which can contribute to depression.

**Bulimia nervosa.** Bulimia nervosa also involves problems with body image and fear of becoming fat. Individuals with this disorder binge eat and then either vomit or overexercise to make up for their bingeing. They may feel a sense of shame or self-loathing, which can lead to depression.

**Binge-eating disorder.** People with binge-eating disorder lose control of their eating, often when they're experiencing a depressed mood. This affects their self-esteem, which worsens their mood and often triggers another binge-eating episode.

### Body dysmorphic disorder

People with body dysmorphic disorder (BDD) are preoccupied with a real or imagined defect in their appearance. They may check mirrors constantly, use makeup to cover the "defect" or have numerous cosmetic surgeries.

People with BDD often have low self-esteem and feel ashamed, unworthy, defective and embarrassed. Depression affects up to three-fourths of people with BDD.

### Borderline personality disorder

People with borderline personality disorder (BPD) typically have disappointing and unstable relationships, intense fears of abandonment, outbursts of anger and feelings of emptiness. They may partake in risky behaviors, such as gambling, spending money irresponsibly, drinking alcohol excessively and attempting suicide.

This difficult, disabling personality disorder mainly affects women. Depression and anxiety are commonly associated with BPD, and people with the disorder often have a family history of depressive illness. Personality disorders often cause serious personal and work problems, which also can lead to depression.

## Chapter 3

# *The biology of depression*

The many risk factors for depression described in Chapter 2 show that depression can develop for a variety of reasons. It may be difficult to imagine that somehow these factors share a common link. But a growing body of evidence suggests that — directly or indirectly — they all can trigger changes in brain function.

In recent decades, scientists have established that changes in brain activity and depression go hand in hand. But many details remain unclear. Researchers don't know for certain what goes wrong with brain functioning to cause depression and if the pattern is always the same. There may be different causes in different people.

Part of the reason so many questions remain unanswered is that the brain is an incredibly complex organ that's difficult to study. Intensive research will likely provide more information in coming years. Meanwhile, here are some of the key findings to date that have helped researchers and doctors better understand the biology of depression.

## Family, adoption and twin studies

Scientists believe that some people have a vulnerability to depression, just as other people have a vulnerability to cancer or heart disease. This doesn't mean that if one of your parents has or had depression you're destined to get it. Rather, it means that you may have inherited one or more genes that increase your risk of developing depression.

### Families

Many studies have examined depression in families. These studies found that family members of someone who is depressed or has been depressed in the past have a greater likelihood of developing depression. Family histories show that depression commonly passes from one generation to the next.

### Adopted children

Researchers have studied men and women who were adopted as children. They found that adopted individuals whose biological parents experienced depression were more likely to develop depression than adopted individuals whose biological parents didn't experience depression. This contradicted the idea that you "learn" how to be depressed from a depressed parent.

### Identical twins

Research involving twins provides the most convincing evidence that depression has a genetic component. These studies found that when one twin of a pair develops depression, an identical twin is more likely than a fraternal twin to develop the illness too. This is because identical twins have the same genetic makeup, whereas fraternal twins share only some of their genes.

### The search goes on

So far, scientists haven't been able to identify specific genes that increase an individual's risk of depression, but they continue to search. It's doubtful that a single gene will account for depression in most people. More likely, several genes are involved. Identifying those genes associated with depression doesn't necessarily mean that doctors will be able to prevent the illness, but the information could lead to better diagnosis and treatment.

However, if one twin of a pair of identical twins experiences depression, that doesn't mean the other twin is destined to be depressed too. As stated in Chapter 2, among identical twins who experience depression, in only 40 percent of cases do both twins become depressed. This suggests that genes, though important, are only partly responsible for the illness. In addition to genetic make-up, environmental factors play a key role in the development of depression. That's why depression can occur in people with no known family history of the illness.

## Hormone studies

Studies of people who are depressed show that some of them have abnormal amounts of certain hormones in their blood. Researchers believe that an increase or a decrease in the production of specific hormones may interfere with your brain's natural chemistry, leading to depression.

With the exception of thyroid hormone, levels of other hormones aren't routinely measured when diagnosing or treating depression. In certain circumstances, however, your doctor may choose to check other hormone levels.

### Thyroid hormones

When your thyroid glands aren't working properly, one of two types of problems can result:

- Release of too much thyroid hormone (hyperthyroidism)
- Release of too little thyroid hormone (hypothyroidism)

Either condition may lead to depression, but depression tends to be more common with hypothyroidism.

### Adrenal hormones

Your adrenal glands are located near your kidneys and produce several hormones that play a key role in body activities such as metabolism, immune function and stress response. Studies show that some people with depression may have too much of the adrenal hormone cortisol in their blood. Excess cortisol can directly alter brain function or alter your brain's natural balance of chemical messengers (neurotransmitters).

Depression is also a common symptom of Cushing's disease, which results from excess production of adrenal hormones. More commonly, depression is a side effect of treatment with prednisone. Prednisone is a cortisol-like drug used to treat inflammatory conditions, including systemic lupus erythematosus, rheumatoid arthritis and asthma. When treatment of Cushing's disease is complete and cortisol levels return to normal, or when the dosage of prednisone is reduced or the drug discontinued, symptoms of depression often lessen or disappear.

### Stress hormones

Within your brain is an area called the hypothalamus (HI-poh-THAL-ah-mus), which regulates hormone secretion. It manufactures and releases small proteins (peptides) that act on the pituitary gland at the base your brain. These peptides stimulate or inhibit the gland's release of various hormones into your bloodstream. When your brain assesses a potential threat, it alerts what's known as the HPA axis — the hypothalamus, pituitary gland and adrenal glands. They make up the hormonal system that regulates your body's response to stress. The HPA axis releases a variety of hormones, including cortisol, to help you challenge the threat or to move out of harm's way.

Many studies show that people with depression have increased activity of the HPA axis. This can be a problem in that some areas of your brain are sensitive to the activity of stress hormones. Excess hormones may impair your memory and your ability to function. The increase in cortisol and other hormones during periods of stress — especially during chronic stress or an episode of severe stress — is thought to disrupt your brain's natural chemistry, increasing your risk of depression.

### Sex hormones

The sex hormones estrogen (female) and testosterone (male) affect everything from sex drive to memory. They influence how you feel, how you think and how you behave. Sex hormones also appear to provide protection against a variety of illnesses, including depression. Although the links between sex hormones and depression aren't yet well understood, trouble may begin for some people when levels of these hormones drop.

**Estrogen.** Women are at a higher risk of depression than are men, and the hormone estrogen may be one reason why. Estrogen is thought to alter the activity of neurotransmitters that contribute to depression. Many women experience a dip in mood during the premenstrual phase of their monthly cycles. Some suffer from postpartum depression following the birth of a baby. Others experience depression during the time around menopause. These are all times when estrogen levels typically decrease.

**Testosterone.** Once men hit midlife, they may face an increased risk of depression. A decrease in the male hormone testosterone may be a contributing factor. Testosterone levels peak in men at age 20 and then slowly decline. The decrease becomes more significant beyond age 50. Information on the relationship between testosterone and depression is scanty. At best, researchers suggest there's some evidence of a connection between testosterone levels and depression in some men. The importance of that connection is yet to be determined.

## Brain imaging studies

Brain imaging technology has allowed researchers to move beyond speculation to actually see what occurs in the brain during periods of depression. Advanced imaging techniques — especially positron emission tomography (PET) — make it possible for researchers to compare brain activity during periods of depression with brain activity in nondepressed periods. (See page 3 of the color section that follows this chapter.) The comparison is done in a variety of ways, including measuring oxygen and blood sugar (glucose) use. The more active an area of the brain is, the more oxygen and glucose its tissues require.

Studies comparing groups of depressed and nondepressed people show that depressed people have less activity in certain

### Enriched beginnings stimulate brain circuitry

At birth you have trillions of nerve cells (neurons) in your brain waiting to be fired up and put to work. If they're used, they connect with other neurons and become part of your brain's circuitry. Those that aren't used may be lost.

Regions of your brain mature at different times. By the time you reach adolescence, your emotional circuitry is mature. So what you learn up to that point is critical. Studies indicate that growing up in an enriched environment — one filled with positive social interaction and opportunities to learn — generally leads to better brain structure and function. This, in turn, is thought to result in a greater capacity to cope with stress and emotions.

Children who experience abuse or neglect stand a greater chance of experiencing depression as an adult. Stress and constant threats may interfere with the development of their emotional circuits. When a child is frequently on high alert because of stress — when more circuits than normal are searching for impending danger — certain areas of the brain may develop differently. This can make a child more sensitive to stress and depression, even into his or her adult years.

Fortunately, the effects of severe or persistent early stress may be reversible. Studies show that children who experienced trauma in early childhood may still thrive if they're subsequently placed in an enriched, caring environment. Children also model themselves on how adults around them respond to stress. If a parent or other adult exhibits healthy responses to stress, the child is more likely to learn these as well.

brain regions than people who aren't depressed. This suggests depression is related to changes in the function of certain cells.

From brain imaging studies researchers have also been able to witness the brain's unique ability to change, even in adulthood. For example, images comparing brain activity and function before and after different types of treatment can show noticeable differences. In relation to depression this means that with the help of treatment your brain can change to operate in a healthier manner.

# Medication studies

Researchers often learn a great deal about illnesses by accident. Another important clue to the biology of depression came about thanks to a drug called reserpine developed to treat high blood pressure. A number of people who took reserpine became depressed. To learn why reserpine caused depression and to gain a better understanding of brain chemistry during depression, scientists studied the effects of the drug on brain activity. Their findings and the results of other drug studies revealed the association between depression and brain chemicals called neurotransmitters.

### Brain neurotransmitters

Imagine your brain is like a large computer network. All of its regions are interconnected by a complex system of transmission lines. In reality, the transmission lines are nerve bundles. The tips of these bundles contain neurotransmitters that serve as data messengers between nerve cells (neurons).

The nerve cells release neurotransmitters into a small gap (synapse) between a sending nerve cell and a receiving nerve cell. The neurotransmitter binds to a receptor on the receiving nerve cell. During the transfer of information, electrical signals from the sending nerve cell are changed into chemical signals that communicate the message to the receiving nerve cell. When the transfer is complete, the receiving cell changes the chemical signals back to electrical signals. (See the illustration on page 5 of the color section.) Communication from one cell to another occurs very rapidly, so your brain can react quickly to the message.

### Neurotransmitters and depression

In the early years of depression research, the neurotransmitter norepinephrine (nor-ep-ih-NEF-rin) was thought to be the most likely transmitter involved in depression. It plays a key role in your emotional responses and is located in regions where brain activity decreases during periods of depression. Scientists concluded that depression results from reduced levels of norepinephrine, and drug companies went to work developing antidepressant medications

## Your brain's mood regulator

Your mood and emotions are influenced by a part of your brain called the limbic system. It's made up of several interconnected structures that process and respond to messages from your senses and thoughts.

An area of your brain that's intricately connected to your limbic system is the hypothalamus, which regulates the release of a variety of hormones into your bloodstream. These hormones affect many aspects of your life, including sleep, appetite, sexual desire and your reaction to stress. That's part of the reason people with depression may not sleep well or may have little appetite. There's a biological link.

that acted primarily to increase the activity of norepinephrine in brain cells.

During the 1980s a new group of antidepressant medications — called selective serotonin reuptake inhibitors (SSRIs) — was introduced. These medications acted primarily on the neurotransmitter serotonin (ser-oh-TOE-nin). Like norepinephrine, serotonin is a mood regulator that's located in brain regions affected by depression.

Levels of norepinephrine and serotonin — and their balance with each other — play a role in how you react to daily life events, such as feeling happy when you see a loved one or crying when you watch a sad movie.

Normally, your brain adjusts so that your emotion properly matches the situation. But when you experience depression, the level of norepinephrine, serotonin or both may be out of sync. They may get stuck in the mode for unhappiness and stay there. As a result you feel sad all of the time, even in situations that you'd normally enjoy.

## Anatomy and physiology

During depression, brain activity changes. Many factors play a role in bringing about these changes. Alterations in brain activity may be related to the genes you inherit from your parents. They may stem from medical conditions, including diseases and disorders that can affect hormone function, such as diseases of the thyroid and adrenal glands or changes in the production of sex gland hormones. Stress, especially if it's severe or persistent, also can produce changes in brain activity, which can trigger depression. In addition to the adrenal glands, your body's stress response system includes parts of the brain called the hypothalamus and the pituitary gland.

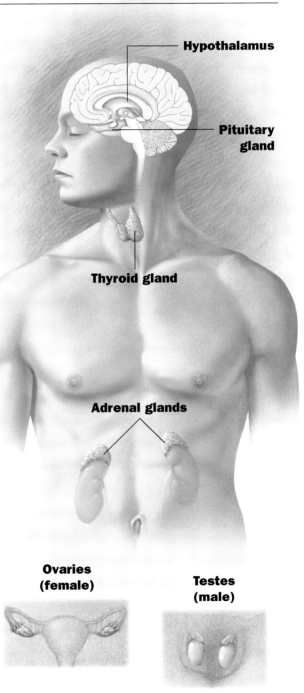

**Hypothalamus**

**Pituitary gland**

**Thyroid gland**

**Adrenal glands**

**Ovaries (female)**

**Testes (male)**

# Brain imaging

**Axial section**

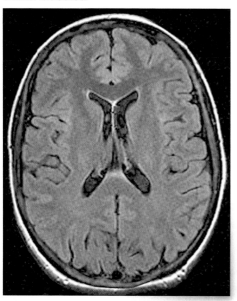

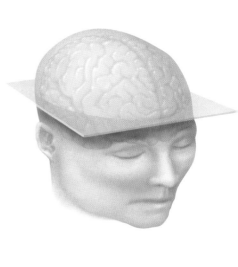

**Sagital section**

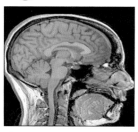

**Coronal section**

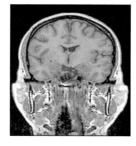

Advances in brain imaging have improved researchers' and doctors' understanding of the biology of depression. The two major types of brain imaging systems are those that show the brain's anatomy and structure, as shown on this page, and those that show the intensity of brain activity, as shown on the opposite page.

# Images of depression

**Not depressed**

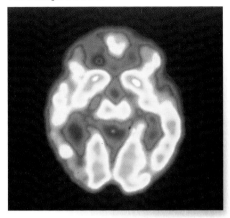

**Depressed**

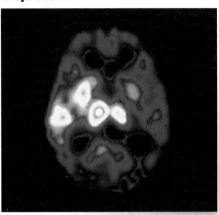

Here's an example of differences in brain activity between a person who isn't depressed and a person experiencing depression. The yellow and orange shading indicates areas of the brain with more brain activity. During depression, brain activity is reduced.

**Depressed**

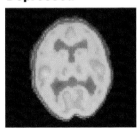

**Mania**

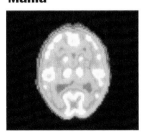

**Depressed**

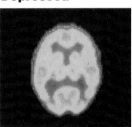

This is an example of an individual with bipolar disorder experiencing rapid changes in mood from depression to mania and back to depression. As you can see, brain activity increases dramatically during mania and then decreases during depression.

Source for upper two images: Anand Kumar, M.D., *Proceedings of the National Academy of Sciences*, 1993, 90:7019-23. Copyright 1993, American Psychiatric Association. Reprinted by permission. Source for lower three images: Louis Baxter, M.D., *Archives of General Psychiatry*, 1985, 42:441-47. Copyright 1985, American Medical Association. Reprinted by permission.

# Neurotransmitters in action: From macro to micro

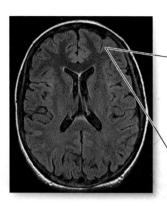

In the microscopic photograph to the right are magnified nerve cells from the area indicated on the magnetic resonance image (MRI) shown above.

Here is the same section of nerve cells further magnified. These cells communicate with one another by way of chemical messengers called neurotransmitters.

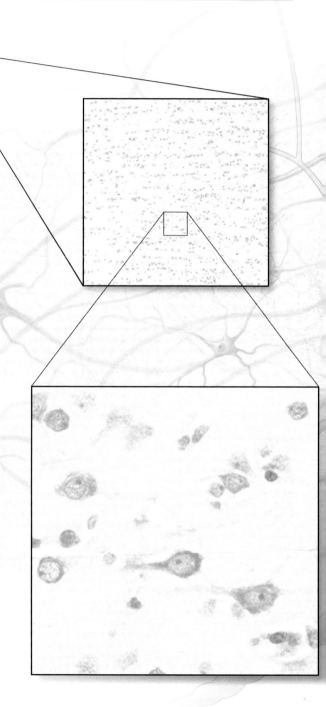

# Neurotransmitters in action:
# How brain cells communicate

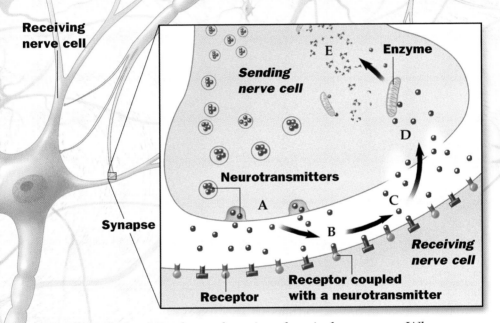

Brain cells communicate by exchanging chemical messages. When a sending nerve cell communicates with a receiving nerve cell, the following steps occur: (A) Cellular packages containing chemical messengers (neurotransmitters) are released into a gap (synapse) between the two cells. (B) In the synapse a neurotransmitter is attracted to and binds with a receptor on the receiving nerve cell. This alters the activity of the receiving nerve cell. (C) Once communication is complete, the neurotransmitter is released back into the synapse. (D) The neurotransmitter remains there until it's taken back within the sending nerve cell, a process called reuptake. (E) In the cell the neurotransmitter is repackaged for future use or broken down by monoamine oxidase enzymes.

## Neurotransmitters and depression

People who are depressed may have a smaller amount of certain neurotransmitters in the gap (synapse) between nerve cells than people who aren't depressed.

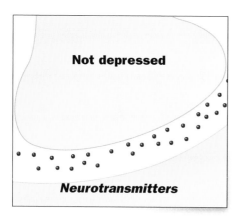

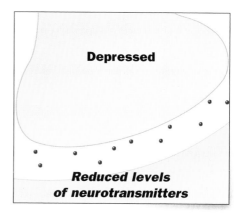

### How antidepressants work

Antidepressant medications work in different ways to treat depression. A common result of all of these approaches is an increase in the level or activity of certain neurotransmitters in the synapse. This causes receiving nerve cells to get messages more like that of people who aren't depressed.

### Neurotransmitter reuptake inhibitors

Some antidepressants work as reuptake inhibitors. They interfere with step D, making it difficult for the neurotransmitters to get back into the sending nerve cell. The neurotransmitters build up in the synapse where they're free to continue binding with receiving nerve cell receptors.

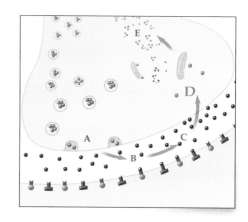

# Neurotransmitters and depression

### Receptor blockers

Some antidepressants work as receptor blockers. One of several ways in which receptor blockers work is by interfering with step B and preventing neurotransmitters from binding with certain receptors. The receiving nerve cell receives fewer messages from the blocked receptors, resulting in a change in the balance of messages transmitted by other receptors that aren't blocked.

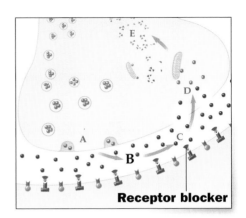

### Enzyme inhibitors

Some antidepressants work as enzyme inhibitors and interfere with step E. Because they can't be broken down by monoamine oxidase enzymes, the neurotransmitters build up within the cell. However, the cell can only store so many neurotransmitters. This causes more neurotransmitters to be present in the synapse, where they're free to continue binding with receiving nerve cell receptors.

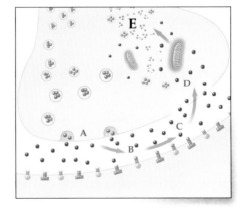

## Depression and aging

Blood vessel changes from high blood pressure, diabetes or high cholesterol may damage small areas of brain tissue. Brain imaging research suggests that older adults with this form of brain tissue damage are more likely to develop depression. Maintaining a healthy weight, exercising regularly, and getting appropriate and timely medical care may help reduce your risk of developing depression as you age.

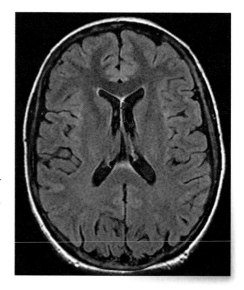

The top image shows a normal brain. The bottom image shows several small areas of brain damage from diseased blood vessels (see arrows).

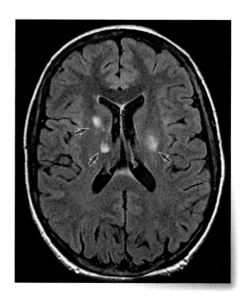

## Chapter 4

# Recognizing and diagnosing depression

Depression often goes unnoticed or untreated. Health care providers may fail to associate physical symptoms such as fatigue, headache, pain or insomnia with depression. And individuals who are depressed often deny or minimize their symptoms, or they rationalize them as just stress. Many people avoid seeing a doctor because they mistakenly associate a diagnosis of depression with a failure of willpower or character. Although the stigma associated with mental illness is lessening, lack of knowledge, worry as to how others will react and concerns about confidentiality still keep people from seeking help.

As depression receives broader acceptance as a medical illness among both doctors and the general public, its recognition and diagnosis are gradually increasing.

## What are the warning signs?

Everyone feels depressed once in a while. The death of a close friend, the end of a relationship, the loss of a job or a move away from home are all normal reasons to feel down. After a short time, most people recover from their despair and once again begin to experience feelings of happiness. It's when those sad, lonely, irritable, tired feelings don't seem to go away that you may be experiencing depression.

Just as depression may be triggered by a stressful event, it can also develop for no apparent reason. Symptoms may come on suddenly, or they may develop slowly over months and years. Signs and symptoms of depression vary and don't always follow a particular pattern. In fact, you can be depressed without even feeling "depressed." Irritability and loss of usual interests or pleasures are other key ways in which depression may express itself.

Depression is characterized by several of the following signs or symptoms:

**Persistent sadness.** You may feel down, sad or empty. You may cry all of the time or report feeling numb — not happy or sad.

**Irritability.** You may be easily irritated and get upset over things that never used to bother you.

**Feelings of anxiety.** You may be unusually nervous, worried or preoccupied with minor concerns — always making mountains out of molehills. You may feel restless or experience stomach upset or the butterflies.

**Loss of interest or pleasure in life.** You may lose the ability to find pleasure in people, hobbies or activities that you previously found enjoyable.

**Neglect of personal responsibilities or personal care.** If you're normally prompt at household, work or school activities, you may forget to pay your bills, fall behind at your job or start cutting classes. You may pay less attention to personal hygiene, such as washing your hair. Women who normally worry about their appearance may start going out without makeup or dress in rumpled clothing.

**Changes in eating habits.** You may not feel hungry and may lose weight without trying. Or you may overeat and gain weight.

**Changes in sleeping patterns.** You may have trouble falling asleep at night, awaken frequently, or wake up early in the morning and not be able to get back to sleep. Or you may sleep too much and spend a good share of the day in bed.

**Fatigue and loss of energy.** You may have a low energy level and feel tired all of the time. Your body movements may slow, and you may talk more slowly.

**Decreased concentration, attention and memory.** You may have trouble concentrating and keeping your mind focused on tasks at work, school or home. Making decisions, even simple ones, becomes more difficult. You forget things easily.

**Extreme mood changes.** You may experience big swings in mood, going from euphoria to despair in a short period of time.

**Feelings of helplessness.** You may feel as if you're no longer in control of your life. You may become easily overwhelmed by stress and more dependent upon other people, even for simple tasks.

**Feelings of hopelessness.** You may have difficulty seeing a bright and positive future and have a sense that things will never get better. Reassurance from others that life will improve doesn't seem to help. Motivating yourself becomes impossible, and you may wonder if life is worth living.

**Feelings of worthlessness or guilt.** You may begin to feel as if you're not as good as people around you, causing you to withdraw from others. You may feel guilty for no particular reason. Something that happened years ago and hasn't bothered you may now become a preoccupation and a guilty burden.

**Continuous negative thinking.** You may become pessimistic, have low self-esteem and not believe that things will get better. Phrases such as, "I'm no good," "I'm not capable," and "What's the point?" may become commonplace.

**Physical symptoms that don't respond to treatment.** You may experience headaches, digestive disorders or chronic pain, which are commonly associated with depression.

**Increased alcohol or drug use.** You may try to seek relief from your depressive symptoms with alcohol, prescription medications or illegal drugs. Because these substances affect brain function, they can make depression worse.

**Thoughts of death or suicide.** You may wish that you were dead and have thoughts such as, "If God would take me, it would be a relief," or "If I could just fall asleep and not wake up, my family would be better off." Or you may experience actual thoughts of killing yourself.

If you find yourself making a suicide plan, seek immediate medical attention. Suicide is discussed in detail in Chapter 15.

**Think you may be depressed? Take a test**

Some mental health organizations offer online self-assessments to help you determine if you may be experiencing depression. One such organization is the National Mental Health Association. You can access its self-assessment survey at the following Web address: *www.depression-screening.org*. The survey is a confidential multiple choice questionnaire to help identify signs and symptoms of depression and to indicate if you should seek further evaluation by a mental health provider. Results are available instantly online.

Another way to help identify if you may be depressed is to complete the questionnaire near the end of this chapter.

## Pathways for getting help

If test results or the way you're feeling suggest that you may be depressed, contact someone who can help. Many people can assist you in getting appropriate medical care and determining if depression is the source of your symptoms.

- Make an appointment with your family doctor.
- Ask family members or friends to recommend a psychiatrist, a psychologist or a counselor.
- Call a local community health organization or a mental health center. They frequently offer free services or services at a reduced cost.
- See your minister or spiritual leader for advice or a referral.
- Contact the local or state branch of mental health professional organizations. See page 185 for a listing of organizations, including their Web addresses.
- Call a local hot line or help line.

## Who provides mental health care?

Your family doctor is the person you may see for most of your health problems. But for some health conditions, it's often helpful to have a specialist involved in treatment. For example, for treatment of arthritis, you may want to see an arthritis specialist (rheumatologist). To control your diabetes, your doctor may refer you to a diabetes specialist (endocrinologist). But what about depression? Who treats depression? And how do you know the type of professional you need?

Following is a list of health care providers trained to treat depression. If your symptoms are mild, your family doctor may be able to treat your illness. But if your symptoms are severe, if your depression is interfering with your ability to function on a daily basis or if your current treatment doesn't seem to be working, then you should see a specialist.

When choosing a mental health care provider, consider issues of education, licensing, areas of specialization, fees, office hours and the expected length of treatment.

### Psychiatrist

A psychiatrist is a medical doctor who has completed at least 4 years of specialty training after earning a medical degree (M.D.). Psychiatrists are licensed to practice medicine in the state in which they work, and they're certified by the American Board of Psychiatry and Neurology. Psychiatrists are the most medically trained providers of mental health care. They're qualified to perform many aspects of treatment for depression, including prescribing medication.

### Psychologist

A psychologist typically has completed at least 4 years of graduate training and, in most states, holds a doctorate degree (Ph.D., Psy.D. or Ed.D.) in psychology. Graduate programs in professional psychology are accredited by the American Psychological Association. Some states allow individuals who have a master's degree in psychology to practice under the supervision of a Ph.D. or an M.D.

Psychologists administer psychological tests to diagnose depression, and they use various forms of psychotherapy to treat the illness. Psychotherapy involves discussing fears and concerns, dealing with emotions, and changing behaviors. Unlike psychiatrists, psychologists aren't able to prescribe medications. All states license psychologists, and the American Board of Professional Psychology certifies psychologists.

### Social worker

According to the National Association of Social Workers, clinical social workers are the largest group of professionally trained mental health care providers in the United States. Clinical social workers hold a master's degree in social work and are trained to practice psychotherapy. Most states require that they be licensed or certified by the state in which they practice. Clinical social workers work in a variety of settings, such as hospitals, outpatient clinics and social service agencies. They cannot prescribe medications. Not all social workers in mental health services are licensed to practice psychotherapy. Some work as case managers, coordinating psychiatric, medical and other services for people who need help managing certain aspects of their lives.

### Psychiatric nurse

A psychiatric nurse holds a degree in nursing, is licensed as a registered nurse (R.N.) and has additional training in psychiatry. A clinical nurse specialist (C.N.S.) has a bachelor's degree in nursing, is licensed as an R.N., and holds a master's degree in mental health nursing or a related field. Clinical nurse specialists can provide psychotherapy. In some states, once certified, they can prescribe psychiatric medications, usually under the supervision of a physician. Nurse practitioners (N.P.) also work in psychiatry. They have advanced training in physical assessment skills, physiology, pharmacology and physical diagnosis, and they can prescribe medications.

### Family therapist

Family therapists are licensed professionals, including psychiatrists, psychologists, social workers and nurses, who receive additional training in family therapy. They diagnose and treat mental illness within the context of relationships. Members of the American Association for Marriage and Family Therapy have a master's, doctorate or medical degree, and 2 years of supervised practice.

### Pastoral counselor

A pastoral counselor is a member of the clergy who integrates religious concepts with training in the behavioral sciences. Licensing is not required to serve as a pastoral counselor. However, pastoral counselors may seek certification from the American Association of Pastoral Counselors.

## Where to start?

If you think you may be depressed, make an appointment with your primary care doctor, if you have one, or a mental health professional. Your primary care doctor can provide you guidance and may be able to diagnose and treat your depression. For mild to moderate symptoms, a social worker, a psychiatric nurse or a family therapist also may be able to provide the care you need.

See a psychiatrist or a psychologist if your symptoms are severe, if your depression is interfering with your ability to function on a daily basis, if your current treatment doesn't seem to be working, or if your family doctor or another health care professional refers you. If you're presently undergoing treatment for depression, but the treatment doesn't seem to be helping you, consider getting a second opinion.

More often than in the past, today a team of professionals, including a psychiatrist, a psychologist, a social worker or a psychiatric nurse, may work together to give you the best care possible in the most cost-effective manner. Select an individual or a group with whom you feel comfortable. If you ever begin to feel uncomfortable about your treatment, don't be afraid to seek a second opinion.

## Steps to diagnosis

Once you've made an appointment with a mental health professional, what can you expect? Sometimes he or she can determine in just one visit if you're experiencing depression. In other cases — especially when depression is accompanied by another illness or by

## Sample patient questionnaire

Here's a patient questionnaire used by some Mayo Clinic primary care doctors to help diagnose depression.

1. Over the last 2 weeks how often have you been bothered by the following problems?

|  | Not at all | Several days | More than half the days | Nearly every day |
|---|---|---|---|---|
|  | 0 | 1 | 2 | 3 |
| A. Little interest or pleasure in doing things? | ___ | ___ | ___ | ___ |
| B. Feeling down, depressed or hopeless? | ___ | ___ | ___ | ___ |
| C. Trouble falling or staying asleep, or sleeping too much? | ___ | ___ | ___ | ___ |
| D. Feeling tired or having little energy? | ___ | ___ | ___ | ___ |
| E. Poor appetite or overeating? | ___ | ___ | ___ | ___ |
| F. Feeling bad about yourself, or that you are a failure or have let yourself or your family down? | ___ | ___ | ___ | ___ |
| G. Trouble concentrating on things, such as reading the newspaper or watching television? | ___ | ___ | ___ | ___ |
| H. Moving or speaking so slowly that other people have noticed. Or the opposite, being so fidgety or restless that you have been moving around a lot more than usual? | ___ | ___ | ___ | ___ |
| I. Thoughts that you would be better off dead or of hurting yourself in some way? | ___ | ___ | ___ | ___ |

**Total Score:**_____

2. If you've checked off any question on this questionnaire, how difficult have these problems made it for you to do your work, take care of things at home or get along with other people?

___Not difficult      ___Somewhat difficult    ___Very difficult    ___Extremely difficult

Source: PRIME-MD Patient Health Questionnaire

For information on how to score the test, see page 48.

complicated life circumstances — it may take more than one visit before a diagnosis can be made with confidence.

Beyond determining if you're depressed, it's important to identify which type of depression you have. Not all forms of depression respond to treatment in the same way. To best treat your condition, your health care provider needs to understand the type of depression you have. Diagnosing depression may include one or more of the following steps.

### Consultation and medical history

During the first visit, your health care provider will likely ask you to tell him or her about your symptoms, how you're feeling and what your concerns are. He or she may also ask you for your medical history. You can expect questions like, "Have you ever been depressed or felt similarly in the past?" or "Have you experienced other health problems lately?" You may also be asked about the health of your family members.

### Physical examination and tests

If you're seeing your family doctor or a psychiatrist, he or she may perform a physical examination and may request blood tests to check for other medical conditions that may be causing your symptoms. Blood tests help assess the health of your liver and kidneys and identify conditions such as thyroid and adrenal disease, anemia, and infection, all of which can cause depression.

### Personal questionnaire

Some health care professionals use questionnaires to learn more about your specific signs and symptoms, how long you've experienced them and how much they interfere with your daily life. A variety of questionnaires and psychological tests can help diagnose depression. Some are short, others are long. The answers you provide can help identify personal issues that may be relevant to your depression and help determine the severity of your depression. Sometimes questionnaires may be used to measure your progress during treatment.

## Scoring the test

The questionnaire on page 46 can be scored in several ways. One way is as follows:

- Count the number of times that you responded "More than half the days" or "Nearly every day".
- Look to see if you responded "More than half the days" or "Nearly every day" to question A or B.

If you selected "More than half the days" or "Nearly every day" three or more times, including in response to question A or B or both, you may be depressed and should see your doctor. Also see your doctor if you have concerns about depression regardless of how you scored on this test.

## Chapter 5

# Types of depression

Depression can take many forms. What differentiates these forms are the symptoms and circumstances associated with each, along with the duration and severity of the symptoms. However, there often isn't a clear distinction between the different types of depression. They frequently share many of the same characteristics. It's also possible to have more than one type of mood disorder.

In order to determine the treatment that best addresses your particular symptoms and circumstances, mental health professionals classify the various forms of depression. Classification begins with the main categories of depression:

- Major depression
- Dysthymia
- Adjustment disorders
- Bipolar disorders

Within each of these main categories are several subtypes.

## Major depression

Major depression is the most common form of depression. It's characterized by a mood change that lasts more than 2 weeks and

includes one or both of the primary signs of depression:
- Overwhelming feelings of sadness or grief
- Loss of interest or pleasure in usually enjoyable activities

People with major depression also experience at least four of the following signs and symptoms regularly, if not daily:
- Significant weight loss or gain
- Sleep disturbance
- Slowed or restless movement
- Fatigue or loss of energy
- Low self-esteem or inappropriate guilt
- Feelings of worthlessness or guilt
- Feelings of helplessness or hopelessness
- Impaired thinking or concentration
- Loss of sexual desire
- Recurrent thoughts of death or suicide

You may experience major depression only once, or it may return. After your first bout of major depression, you have more than a 50 percent chance of having it again. The odds of recurrence go up with each episode. If you have it twice, the odds jump to 70 percent you'll experience a third episode.

If not treated, episodes of major depression typically last from 6 to 18 months. Early treatment may keep depression from becoming more severe. Continuing treatment can keep depression from coming back.

Major depression may occur with other mental illnesses, such as anxiety or eating disorders. The first episode may begin at any age, but it's most likely to occur between the ages of 25 and 44. Major depression is more common in women than in men. Stressful life events and significant losses are two common triggers for this type of depression.

## Dysthymia

Dysthymia (dis-THI-me-uh) is a long-lasting form of mild depression characterized by a persistently gloomy outlook. The term originates from the Greeks who thought that the thymus gland was at the root of all emotions. Hence, *dys*, meaning "bad," and *thymia*, denoting "a condition of the mind."

Dysthymia generally lasts for at least 2 years and sometimes more than 5 years. It usually isn't disabling, and periods of dysthymia may alternate with brief intervals of feeling normal. Dysthymia can interfere with your work and your social life. In fact, many people with this condition become socially withdrawn and less productive. You have a greater risk of developing major depression if you have dysthymia. When major depression complicates dysthymia, the condition is called double depression.

Signs and symptoms of dysthymia are like those of major depression but not as intense, and you may not experience as many of them. They may include:

- Difficulty concentrating or making decisions
- Social withdrawal
- Irritability
- Restlessness or sluggishness
- Problems sleeping
- Weight loss or gain

Some people with dysthymia recall first experiencing feelings of depression in childhood or adolescence. A few people develop dysthymia after age 50, many times following a medical illness. At least 75 percent of the people with dysthymia have other health problems.

## Adjustment disorders

Adjustment disorders often precede major depression. Let's say your marriage falls apart, your business fails, or you receive a diagnosis of cancer. It's perfectly understandable to feel tense, sad, overwhelmed or angry. Eventually, most people come to terms with the lasting consequences of these life stresses, but some people don't. This is what's known as an adjustment disorder — when your response to a stressful event or situation causes signs and symptoms of depression, but the signs and symptoms aren't strong enough to meet the criteria for major depression.

Doctors typically use these criteria in diagnosing an adjustment disorder:

- Emotional or behavioral symptoms that are in response to an identifiable event that has occurred within the last 3 months.
- The response to the event exceeds the reaction one would typically expect.
- The symptoms aren't due solely to bereavement.

Adjustment disorders can affect anybody. They often occur at times in your life when you may be more vulnerable — when you move away from your parents or at the end of a fulfilling career. Age also is important. For instance, losing your business at age 30 may be less stressful than at age 50, when job prospects may be more limited. Some people develop an adjustment disorder in response to a single event. Among others, it stems from a combination of stressors.

There are several different types of adjustment disorders. An acute adjustment disorder refers to signs and symptoms that last less than 6 months. When symptoms persist, the condition is known as a chronic adjustment disorder. Adjustment disorders are also classified according to primary symptoms:

- Adjustment disorder with depressed mood
- Adjustment disorder with anxiety
- Adjustment disorder with mixed anxiety and depressed mood
- Adjustment disorder with mixed disturbance of emotions and conduct

Age often plays a role in the type of adjustment disorder people experience. Adults typically become depressed or anxious. Adolescents tend to act out their problems. This may include skipping school, using drugs, vandalizing property or some other type of uncharacteristic behavior.

## Bipolar disorders

Some people with depression have recurring cycles of depression and euphoria (mania). This illness, which includes emotions at both extremes (poles), is also known as manic depression or manic-depressive disorder.

In contrast to depression, in a manic phase you feel energetic and unstoppable. You might spend money recklessly or make unwise decisions. You may come up with grandiose ideas that result in everything from a bad business deal to promiscuous behavior. Some people have bursts of increased creativity and productivity during the manic phase.

Signs and symptoms of mania include:
- Abnormal or excessive elation
- Markedly increased energy
- Decreased need for sleep
- Unusual irritability
- Unrealistic beliefs in one's ability and powers
- Increased talkativeness
- Racing thoughts
- Poor judgment
- Enhanced sexual desire
- Provocative, intrusive or aggressive social behavior
- Abuse of alcohol or other drugs

Bipolar disorder isn't as common as major depression or dysthymia. Of the 18 million Americans with depression, about 2 million to 3 million have bipolar disorder. Both men and women are equally at risk of this illness. It typically emerges in adolescence or young adulthood and continues to occur intermittently throughout life. It also tends to run in families. In fact, 80 percent to 90 percent of people who have bipolar disorder have a close relative with some form of depression.

Signs and symptoms of bipolar disorder tend to become more severe over time. You may start out with episodes of depression, mania, or a mixture of both depressed and manic symptoms, separated by "normal" periods with no symptoms. Over time, bipolar episodes become more frequent with shorter normal periods. Severe depression or elation may be accompanied by psychosis, including hallucinations and delusions.

As with other forms of depression, it's critical to get proper treatment for bipolar disorder to prevent worsening illness and to decrease the risk of suicide.

### Varied forms

There are three types of bipolar disorder:

**Bipolar I disorder.** Bipolar I disorder almost always includes one or more periods of major depression and at least one manic or mixed episode. Bipolar I disorder may start with either major depression or mania. If you experience depression first, an episode of mania typically will occur 1 to 2 years later.

**Bipolar II disorder.** With this form of the illness, you have one or more episodes of major depression and at least one period of hypomania, a condition of mild or toned down elation. Your highs aren't as extreme as those of someone with bipolar I disorder. Another difference is the length of intervals between episodes. When you have bipolar II disorder, hypomania often occurs right before or immediately after a period of major depression. There usually isn't a "normal" period in between.

**Cyclothymic disorder.** This is a milder form of bipolar disorder that's chronic. It's characterized by swings between short periods of mild depression to short periods of hypomania. Changes in mood can occur as often as every few days, with cycles continuing for at least 2 years. With cyclothymia, you're never symptom free for more than 2 months at a time, but you're also less likely to develop major depression.

### What's a nervous breakdown?

The term *nervous breakdown* is one that's often used by the general public to describe someone who's experiencing a severe form of mental illness. Most often, an individual said to be having a nervous breakdown is experiencing an episode of major depression or mania. The symptoms are so pronounced that the individual isn't able to function normally and may even be hospitalized. Because symptoms can sometimes appear suddenly, it may seem as though that person is breaking down. Hallucinations and delusions also may accompany severe depression or mania.

Fortunately, with proper diagnosis and treatment, many people who suffer a nervous breakdown are able to recover and return to their earlier quality of life.

# Other dimensions of depression

In addition to identifying the type of depression you have, your doctor will want to consider the severity of your illness and its pattern of symptoms. This helps determine the most effective form of treatment. There are several subtypes of depression. Some of these occur frequently, others are rare.

### Mild to severe depression

Major depression can range from mild to severe. Mild depression involves symptoms that aren't intense and that only minimally interfere with daily life and relationships. Moderate depression includes more intense symptoms and more disruption of work, school, family and relationships. Severe depression implies a large number of depressive symptoms and a significant interference in daily activities. In extreme cases, people with severe depression may be unable to work or care for themselves.

### Suicidal depression

Suicidal depression refers to symptoms so severe that an individual contemplates suicide or makes an attempt on his or her life.

### Acute or chronic depression

Depression can be categorized by the duration of its symptoms. If the symptoms last for a short, clearly defined period, the depression is called acute. If symptoms have been ongoing for more than 6 months, the depression is considered chronic.

### Single episode or recurrent depression

Depression is also categorized based on its pattern over time. A single episode of depression means that you have no prior history of depression. As its name implies, recurrent depression refers to more than one episode of depression.

Both single episode and recurrent depression may be triggered by a particular event. Recurrent depression also may be triggered by a particular season (see "Seasonal affective disorder" on page 57).

## Melancholic depression

*Melancholia* is the term for a type of major depression with certain features. These include an inability to enjoy everyday activities — even if something good happens — loss of appetite, early morning awakenings, slowed movements and unfounded guilt.

## Catatonic depression

Catatonia is an infrequent condition that can occur with depression. During severe depression or mania, some people reach a point where they barely move or move excessively, assume unusual postures, and speak very little. Other features of catatonia include staring, grimacing and repeating words or phrases senselessly.

## Atypical depression

People with atypical depression are still able to experience joy, even if it's only fleeting. But they tend to be highly sensitive to rejection, eat and sleep more than usual, and generally feel fatigued. Atypical depression usually first occurs in adolescence or young adulthood and may be chronic. It is discussed further in Chapter 13.

## Psychotic depression

Psychotic depression is a less common form of the illness. People who experience psychotic depression may hallucinate or experience delusions. Delusions are false beliefs that persist despite evidence to the contrary. In psychotic depression, delusions may be paranoid, financial or medical in nature. People with paranoia are often suspicious and concerned about the intent of those around them. People with financial delusions have an unfounded belief that they are impoverished. People with medical delusions have an unfounded belief that they have a serious medical illness.

## Postpartum depression

Many women experience temporary feelings of sadness following childbirth. These so-called baby blues tend to gradually diminish and usually don't require treatment. Some women, however, experience a form of major depression following childbirth called postpartum depression. Compared with the baby blues, the symptoms are more severe and persistent. An episode of postpartum depression increases the odds that you'll have recurrent bouts of depression, either after subsequent births or at other times.

### Seasonal affective disorder

*Seasonal affective disorder* (SAD) is the term for depressive periods that are related to a change of season. No one knows for certain what causes SAD. Scientists first thought that reduced levels of sunlight increased brain levels of melatonin. Melatonin is a mood-controlling hormone normally produced during darkness. However, studies on the role of melatonin are inconclusive. Some researchers now believe that a lack of sunlight disrupts your circadian rhythms, which regulate your body's internal clocks. This theory may have some merit because there's evidence that SAD is more common in places where daylight hours are limited. People with SAD usually notice mood changes starting in late fall with improvement in spring, but some people experience summer depression, which usually begins in late spring or early summer.

SAD is four times as common in women as in men. The average age of onset is 23, with decreasing risk as you get older. You may have SAD if you've experienced depression and related symptoms during at least two consecutive winters, followed by nondepressed periods in the spring and summer.

## Additional terms

Doctors use other terms to identify and diagnose depression based on its origin and association with other illnesses.

### Secondary depression

Sometimes depression isn't the primary health problem. Rather it's a symptom of another condition. This is known as secondary depression, or depression due to a specific medical condition. Secondary depression may result from diseases of the thyroid or the adrenal gland. Or it may be related to the ongoing effects of heart disease, diabetes or other medical conditions.

## Comorbid depression

Comorbid depression refers to depression that's accompanied by another mental illness. For instance, depression and anxiety commonly occur together. When combined, they can cause more severe signs and symptoms than either alone, and treating both disorders can be challenging. Comorbid depression also includes substance-induced depression — depression that results from the abuse of alcohol, prescription drugs or illegal drugs. Various types of comorbid depression are discussed in Chapter 14.

## Getting it right

Sometimes, determining the type of depression an individual has is fairly easy. The signs and symptoms and the circumstances of that person's life all point to one type of depressive illness. Other times, when several symptoms overlap or a person's life circumstances are more complex, determining the type can be difficult.

To effectively treat your illness, it's important that your doctor know the type of depression you have. Some medications and therapies work better for certain types of depression than for others. In addition, if your depression is accompanied by another mental illness, your doctor will want to take steps to treat both conditions. Treating just depression may not cure the other disorder. And because the other disorder lingers, you're at significant risk of recurring depression.

# Part 2

## Treating Depression

## Chapter 6

# A treatment overview

For most people struggling with depression, help is available. Antidepressant medications and other treatments often can make an astonishing difference in depressive symptoms within a few weeks. With the right treatment, approximately 8 out of 10 people with depression improve. When you consider how poorly depression was treated just 100 years ago, researchers have made remarkable progress in controlling this illness. And there's every indication the future will bring even greater advances.

## A century of progress

Before the 20th century, most people experiencing depression went without a diagnosis and treatment. Early, crude forms of sedatives were given to people with severe agitation, anxiety or psychotic depression, but specific, effective treatments for depression weren't available. For most people, care — if any — was provided by family members. Some people attempted to cure depression with a range of obscure treatments that almost always failed. Often, people with severe, disabling depression were hospitalized in mental asylums until their depression improved, which typically took many months, or even longer.

It was in the mid- to late 1800s that the understanding of depression took a turn toward science. Hoping to better understand mental illnesses, researchers began classifying the illnesses, including depression, according to specific symptoms and clinical features. One of the first major advances from these classification efforts was to distinguish manic-depressive disorder, today called bipolar disorder, from the mental illness schizophrenia. This approach of distinguishing conditions using symptoms and clinical features continues today, but in more sophisticated forms.

As researchers came to better understand the different forms of mental illness, treatments for depression began to emerge.

### 1900s: Psychoanalysis

In 1917 Sigmund Freud published *Mourning and Melancholia*, a book in which he describes depression as "anger turned upon the self." Freud and others theorized that depression could be cured with an intense treatment regime called psychoanalysis. This regime, which included talking about childhood experiences, dream analysis and free association, included sessions that would run about an hour and would occur one to several times a week for months or, sometimes, years. During the first half of the 20th century, psychoanalysis dominated the public's perception of psychiatric treatment.

### 1930s: Electroconvulsive therapy

Researchers once thought that people with seizure disorders (epilepsy) had fewer mental health problems than people who didn't experience seizures. Based on this belief researchers explored whether inducing a seizure could treat mental illness in people without epilepsy. This led to the beginning of what has become known as electroconvulsive therapy (ECT). To treat depression and other mental illnesses, doctors would inject individuals with chemical substances that caused them to have a seizure. Although the seizures often were quite effective in improving symptoms, many people found them terrifying. In addition, using chemical substances to trigger a seizure was unreliable.

In 1938 two Italian physicians were the first to use electrical current instead of chemicals to trigger a seizure in an individual with mental illness. This method, often referred to as shock therapy, was an improvement over earlier methods because it offered greater control of when the seizure would occur. It also had less risk of medical complications, including death. ECT became the first effective treatment for severe depression and by the mid-1950s was used quite commonly.

### Early 1950s: First generation antidepressants

Two unexpected discoveries in the early 1950s led to dramatic changes in the treatment of depression, on a par with the discovery of antibiotics to treat infections and insulin to treat diabetes.

As drug manufacturers searched for new and better antihistamines that didn't cause sedation, one of their discoveries was the medication imipramine (Tofranil). During their research, scientists found that imipramine also improved mood in depressed people who were taking the drug to control allergies or inflammation. Doctors soon began using imipramine to treat depression, along with other medications made from related chemicals. These early antidepressants are known as tricyclics.

The second discovery arose from treatment for tuberculosis. Doctors noticed that a tuberculosis drug called iproniazid elevated moods in some people with tuberculosis who were depressed. Iproniazid became the first in the class of antidepressants called monoamine oxidase inhibitors (MAOIs). The downfall of iproniazid was that it caused serious side effects, especially liver damage, and therefore it was eventually discontinued. However, improved monoamine oxidase inhibitors were developed in its place.

### Late 1950s: Psychotherapy

Because of the time and cost associated with psychoanalysis, psychiatrists and psychologists began exploring alternative approaches to treating depression. Some mental health professionals also felt that psychoanalysis wasn't necessary for treating most cases of depression — that less intense approaches could be just as effective.

These exploration efforts eventually led to the development of two common forms of psychotherapy still used today: cognitive behavior therapy and interpersonal therapy. Cognitive behavior therapy focuses on identifying unhealthy, negative beliefs and behaviors contributing to depression and replacing them with healthy, positive ones. Interpersonal therapy assists people in developing strategies for dealing with relationship and communication problems associated with their depression.

### 1970s: Lithium

An Australian psychiatrist first discovered the benefits of lithium in 1949, but U.S. doctors didn't begin using this drug to treat bipolar disorder until the early 1970s. Lithium acts as a mood stabilizer, treating and preventing the extremes of both mania (elation) and depression. However, it's more effective for treatment of mania.

Before the use of lithium, antidepressants were the only treatment for bipolar depression, but they could trigger a manic phase. Combining lithium with an antidepressant lessens the risk of this side effect.

### Early 1980s: Light therapy

A new subtype of depression called seasonal affective disorder (SAD) — along with its innovative treatment — was first described in medical journals in the early 1980s. SAD affects people who live in higher latitudes, and it occurs during those months when daylight is limited. Treatment for the disorder involves sitting near specialized devices that give off bright light. Studies suggest that bright light therapy may also be effective for other types of depression, especially those with a seasonal component.

### Late 1980s: Second generation antidepressants

It was the discovery of newer classes of antidepressants during the last part of the 1980s that revolutionized the treatment of depression. Selective serotonin reuptake inhibitors (SSRIs) were the first of these medications to be available in the United States. Other types soon followed. Second generation antidepressants aren't necessarily more effective than earlier antidepressants, but they're safer to use, and they produce milder, more tolerable side effects. Because of these improvements, doctors are more willing to prescribe medication for depression, and people are more willing to take it.

### 1990s: Combined medication and psychotherapy

Until the early 1990s, there were two opposing camps when it came to treatment of depression — one camp pressing for medication as the mainstay of treatment, the other for psychotherapy. Several studies helped resolve this struggle. They found that if the two approaches are combined, response to treatment improves, and there's less risk of recurrence. If you have mild to moderate depression, it's not possible to predict if you'll get better from medication alone, psychotherapy alone or a combination of the two. But it is known that for severe or chronic depression, the best chance of improvement is with a combined approach.

### On the horizon

A popular area of study today involves procedures that could one day become alternatives to electroconvulsive therapy. One approach uses magnetic pulses instead of electricity to stimulate areas of the brain affected by depression. A different type of treatment stimulates the vagus nerve, a large nerve in your neck that sends signals to parts of your brain associated with depression.

Another area of research that holds exciting promise for many diseases and disorders, including depression, is genetics. Using genetic information, doctors may be able to tailor medications, selecting drugs that will have a high probability of effectiveness based on an individual's genetic makeup. This has already been shown possible in some people with high blood pressure. Genetic knowledge may even permit early identification of men and women at risk of depression, allowing for early — and possibly preventive — treatment.

## One treatment doesn't fit all

From medications to psychotherapy, there are many options for treating depression, and each plays an important role. Just as the cause of depression may be related to a complex interplay of factors, finding the most effective treatment for your illness may be a complex process that takes time and professional guidance.

In the four chapters that follow, we discuss in greater detail the various options for treating depression, how they work, and their benefits and disadvantages. We also discuss what you can do on a daily basis — in addition to treatment from your doctor — to manage depression or prevent its return.

## Chapter 7

# Medications and how they work

Antidepressant medications are often the first choice in treatment for depression because they're effective and because newer antidepressants produce fewer side effects than earlier medications. There are many types of antidepressants. Scientists don't know exactly how these medications improve symptoms of depression, and the mechanism may be different in different people. It is known that antidepressants influence the activity of brain chemicals called neurotransmitters.

As powerful and effective as these drugs are, though, they aren't always effective. In addition, the medications don't work to the same degree in everyone. Some people may benefit greatly from a certain antidepressant, others only partially and others not at all. Sometimes another type of antidepressant or a combination of medications is necessary to relieve depression.

## Types of antidepressants

To understand the many types of antidepressants that are available, it's helpful to organize them into groups that highlight their similarities and differences. This grouping may be done in several ways: according to when the medications came into use (older vs. newer antidepressants), their chemical structure or their effects on brain neurotransmitters. In this book we discuss antidepressants based on their effects on brain neurotransmitters.

## Brain neurotransmitters

Neurotransmitters are chemicals used by nerve cells to communicate with one another. Nerve cells don't actually touch one another. Therefore, for one nerve cell in the brain to communicate with another nerve cell, the following process takes place: A nerve cell that's sending a message to another nerve cell releases many copies of the same neurotransmitter into a narrow gap (synapse) between the two cells (see illustration on page 5 of the color section).

In the synapse, the neurotransmitters are attracted to and bind with receptors on the receiving nerve cell, much like a key (neurotransmitter) and its lock (receptor). These receptors are located on the outer coating of the receiving nerve cell. When the neurotransmitters bind with the receptors, the receiving nerve cell gets the message from the sending nerve cell. The receiving nerve cell then releases the neurotransmitters back into the synapse, where they remain until they're taken back within the sending nerve cell — a process called reuptake. Inside the sending nerve cell, the neurotransmitters are either repackaged for future use or broken down by an enzyme called monoamine oxidase.

Neurotransmitters associated with depression are serotonin and norepinephrine. A third neurotransmitter, dopamine, also may play a role in the illness. Research suggests depressed people have lower amounts of one or more of these neurotransmitters in the synapses between nerve cells than do people who aren't depressed.

## How antidepressants work

Exactly how antidepressants relieve depression is complex and not fully understood. Doctors believe the medications influence brain activity in three main ways. A specific type of antidepressant may perform one or more of the following actions:

- It may inhibit neurotransmitter reuptake. This keeps the neurotransmitters in the synapse for a longer period, where they remain active and continue triggering messages.

- It may block certain chemical receptors that neurotransmitters act on. This keeps the receiving nerve cell from getting certain messages from the sending nerve cell.
- It may inhibit monoamine oxidase enzymes that break down neurotransmitters. This causes more neurotransmitters to be present in the synapse, where they're free to continue binding with receiving cell receptors.

### 5 categories

Based on their effects on brain neurotransmitters, antidepressants can be divided into five groups:
- Serotonin reuptake inhibitors
- Mixed reuptake inhibitors
- Receptor blockers
- Reuptake inhibitors and receptor blockers
- Enzyme inhibitors

## Serotonin reuptake inhibitors

This group of antidepressants influences the activity of the neuro-transmitter serotonin by blocking serotonin's return (reuptake) to its home cell. The first drugs in this class of medications — called selective serotonin reuptake inhibitors (SSRIs) — were introduced in the late 1980s. The word selective comes from the drugs' ability to work almost exclusively on serotonin and to have little effect on other neurotransmitters. SSRIs include:
- Citalopram (Celexa)
- Fluvoxamine (Luvox)
- Fluoxetine (Prozac)
- Paroxetine (Paxil)
- Sertraline (Zoloft)

Some people who take an SSRI experience gastrointestinal problems. Often these problems are mild and disappear over time. SSRIs can also cause sexual problems. They may reduce sexual desire or prevent an orgasm. About 30 percent of people taking an SSRI report an inability to achieve an orgasm.

An extremely rare but potentially life-threatening side effect of the medications is serotonin syndrome. It most often develops when an SSRI interacts with other antidepressants, usually a monoamine oxidase inhibitor. But it can also occur when SSRIs are taken with other medications that influence serotonin. This is one reason you don't want to take an SSRI with St. John's wort, a nonprescription herbal supplement. St. John's wort causes many chemical actions, one of which affects serotonin activity. Signs and symptoms of serotonin syndrome may include confusion, hallucinations, fluctuations in blood pressure and heart rhythm, fever, seizures, and even coma.

## Mixed reuptake inhibitors

Unlike serotonin reuptake inhibitors, which interfere with the reuptake of only serotonin, mixed reuptake inhibitors block the reuptake of several neurotransmitters.

### Serotonin-norepinephrine reuptake inhibitor
The antidepressant venlafaxine (Effexor) inhibits the reuptake of both serotonin and norepinephrine. Some people who take venlafaxine experience an increase in blood pressure. For this reason, your doctor may closely monitor your blood pressure after you begin taking the medication, especially if you're receiving treatment for high blood pressure.

### Norepinephrine-dopamine reuptake inhibitor
The medication bupropion (Wellbutrin) inhibits the reuptake of both norepinephrine and dopamine. Bupropion is less likely to cause sexual problems or an increase in blood pressure. It's also less likely to cause other common side effects associated with antidepressants, such as drowsiness or weight gain. However, the medication can increase your risk of seizures. Therefore, it generally isn't recommended for people with a history of seizures or people with bulimia nervosa. The eating disorder bulimia nervosa increases risk of seizures.

## Receptor blockers

Instead of inhibiting neurotransmitter reuptake, the antidepressant mirtazapine (Remeron) prevents neurotransmitters from binding with certain nerve cell receptors — mainly those that take messages from the neurotransmitter norepinephrine. This blockade of select receptors is thought to indirectly increase norepinephrine and serotonin activities in your brain.

## Reuptake inhibitors and receptor blockers

These antidepressants act on brain cells in two ways: by inhibiting the reuptake of one or more neurotransmitters and by blocking one or more nerve cell receptors.

### Trazodone
Trazodone (Desyrel) inhibits the reuptake of serotonin and blocks a certain type of serotonin receptor. To a lesser extent it also blocks several types of receptors that receive messages from the neurotransmitters norepinephrine and histamine. Because it blocks histamine receptors, trazodone is more likely than other antidepressants to cause drowsiness (sedation). It's commonly used in low doses as a sleep aid. Sometimes doctors will combine trazodone with another antidepressant. Trazodone helps promote better sleep, while the other medication works to relieve depression.

### Nefazodone
Nefazodone (Serzone) inhibits the reuptake of serotonin and, to a lesser extent, norepinephrine. It also blocks a certain type of serotonin receptor and, to a lesser extent, a certain type of norepinephrine receptor.

### Maprotiline
Maprotiline (Ludiomil) inhibits the reuptake of norepinephrine and blocks certain types of norepinephrine receptors.

### Tricyclic antidepressants

Tricyclic antidepressants inhibit the reuptake of serotonin and nor-epinephrine and block certain receptors. Each type of tricyclic antidepressant works in a slightly different way, establishing its own pattern of effect. Tricyclics include:

- Amitriptyline (Elavil, Endep)
- Desipramine (Norpramin)
- Imipramine (Tofranil)
- Nortriptyline (Aventyl, Pamelor)
- Protriptyline (Vivactil)
- Trimipramine (Surmontil)

Tricyclic antidepressants have been used since the 1950s. However, they're generally not a medication of first choice because they can cause more bothersome side effects than other antidepressants. Tricyclics are most often prescribed when other antidepressants don't work. They can also be beneficial in management of chronic pain. Common side effects of tricyclics include dry mouth, blurred vision, dizziness, drowsiness, weight gain, constipation and difficulty urinating.

Tricyclics may trigger or worsen certain medical conditions, including an enlarged prostate, some forms of glaucoma and some forms of heart disease.

## Enzyme inhibitors

Monoamine oxidase inhibitors (MAOIs) block the action of monoamine oxidase enzymes located inside your nerve cells that break down the neurotransmitters norepinephrine and serotonin. This causes the neurotransmitters to remain active longer in the synapse. MAOIs include:

- Phenelzine (Nardil)
- Tranylcypromine (Parnate)

Because these drugs can cause serious side effects and because so many alternate antidepressants are available, MAOIs are used infrequently today. Doctors generally turn to them when other antidepressants have failed.

Food and drug interactions are a serious concern with MAOIs. Foods and medications that contain high levels of the amino acid tyramine can interact with the medications, causing a spike in blood pressure, which can lead to a headache, a rapid heartbeat and possibly a stroke. People who take MAOIs need to follow a strict diet and be careful about use of other medications. Foods that contain the amino acid tyramine include cheese, chocolate, soy products, some beans, avocados, coffee, beer, red wine and pickles.

When discontinuing an MAOI, it's important to follow dietary and medication restrictions for at least 2 weeks after you stop taking the medication to avoid possible reactions from lingering effects of the drug on your system. Newer, more selective MAOIs that don't carry the risk of food and medication interactions are being explored and may be on the horizon.

## Choosing an antidepressant

Your doctor considers several factors when selecting an antidepressant to treat your depression.

### Effectiveness

All antidepressants approved by the Food and Drug Administration (FDA) have been found to be equally effective, with a 60 percent to 80 percent chance of improving symptoms. Doctors can't predict which medications will or will not be effective for any given person. One clue that can be helpful to your doctor in deciding on a drug is family history. If a close relative had a good response to a certain antidepressant, that antidepressant may also be helpful for you.

### Side effects

In general, newer antidepressants are less likely to cause serious complications, drug interactions and bothersome side effects than are older antidepressants. Newer antidepressants include SSRIs, venlafaxine, mirtazapine and nefazodone. Older antidepressants include tricyclics and MAOIs.

However, even newer medications have the potential for side effects. Common side effects of antidepressants include nausea, headache, diarrhea, fatigue, insomnia, bloating, dizziness, appetite changes, weight fluctuations and nervousness. These effects often are mild and often diminish within several days to a couple of weeks. Doctors can't predict which medications may cause side effects in certain individuals. Why some people have trouble with certain antidepressants and others don't isn't well understood.

In addition to reduced risk of side effects, another advantage of newer antidepressants over older ones is that they're more convenient to take. To reduce unpleasant side effects, older antidepressants often are taken in two or three doses each day, or the dose is gradually increased over a prolonged period. Newer antidepressants generally require that you take them only once a day, and most people reach an effective dose sooner.

Another downfall of some older antidepressants is that when you first begin taking the medication, you need to have your blood checked regularly to ensure you're receiving the proper amount of the drug.

## Cost

Newer medications are generally more expensive than older medications, mainly because older antidepressants are available as generic preparations. A medication usually is introduced as a relatively expensive brand name drug that's sold exclusively by the company that developed it. When the patent for a drug expires — generally 10 to 15 years after it's granted — other companies are allowed to manufacture the drug, producing what are called generic medications. Generics almost always cost less than brand name drugs and are usually just as effective. The FDA regulates the manufacture of generic medications, just as it does brand name drugs. This helps ensure the quality of the product.

If cost is a factor for you, your doctor may initially recommend an older antidepressant available in generic form to see if it can effectively control your symptoms without bothersome side effects. In addition, some health plans or insurance companies provide or reimburse members only for certain types of antidepressants.

## Working in combination

Sometimes two antidepressants are better than one. For example, if an SSRI fails to give you complete relief from your depression, your doctor might add a second medication from another drug family, such as bupropion or mirtazapine.

These drug combinations — with each drug working in a different way — are often able to control depression when one medication by itself isn't effective. However, when you combine drugs you may experience increased side effects or drug interactions, so close monitoring is essential. Once your condition stabilizes for a period of weeks to months, your doctor may drop you back to a single drug, or perhaps reduce the dosages.

When a person is severely depressed, a doctor may prescribe a stimulant, in addition to an antidepressant. Stimulants include the medications methylphenidate (Ritalin, Methylin) and dextroamphetamine (Dexedrine, Dextrostat). Stimulants help boost your mood and energy level during the time it takes an antidepressant to begin working. Typically, after 1 to 4 weeks, you stop taking the stimulant and remain on just the antidepressant.

## Dosage

If you're depressed, you want to get better fast. Your doctor wants the same thing too. Unfortunately, antidepressants don't work immediately. They take time. The medication may begin to work within 2 weeks, but it may take up to 8 weeks before you realize its full effects. If the initial dosage your doctor recommends doesn't work, he or she may want to try a higher dosage. However, each dosage adjustment sets back the clock, and you may need to wait another period of weeks before you know if the new dose is more effective.

Doctors are sometimes tempted to recommend a higher dose of the drug from the start, to get a faster response. But this temptation has to be balanced against the fact that too much of the drug taken too quickly increases the risk of side effects. You may get frustrated with the side effects and want to stop the medication before it has had a chance to work. Or you may end up taking a higher dose of the medication than you actually need, at a greater cost.

## Duration

Drug treatment for depression is often divided into two stages. The initial focus is on getting better. This stage is called acute therapy. The latter focus is on staying well. This stage is called continuation or maintenance therapy.

Some people need to take medication the rest of their life to control their depression and to prevent a relapse. For others, medication is only a temporary treatment until the unknown biological factors that caused the depression resolve, or until the life events that triggered the illness improve. In general, if you have a single episode of depression that continued for several months to years before you sought treatment, once your depression has cleared, continue on an antidepressant at least an additional 6 to 12 months. Discontinuing the drug sooner may increase the chance the depression will return when the medication is stopped.

Decisions regarding how long to continue an antidepressant need to be individualized to each person's circumstances. Factors your doctor will consider include the severity and length of your depression before treatment, how difficult the depression was to treat, whether you've had previous episodes or a family history of depression, if you were experiencing stress before or during your treatment, if you're still experiencing stress, and if you feel equipped to manage your stress.

When it's time to discontinue your antidepressant, you'll want to work with your doctor to gradually reduce the dose of the drug over time. At a lower dose some people find that their symptoms begin to recur, and they need to return to a higher dose of the medication for another 6 to 12 months. In a small percentage of people whose depression recurs after the medication is stopped, the medication isn't effective when tried again. Gradually reducing the dose and watching for recurrent symptoms can help avoid this.

## Additional medications

Depending on the type of depression you have and if your depression is accompanied by another condition, your doctor may recommend a second medication in addition to an antidepressant to treat your illness.

## Mood stabilizers

Mood stabilizers are taken for bipolar disorder, which produces swings between depression and euphoria (mania). The two main types of mood stabilizers are lithium and anticonvulsants.

**Lithium.** Lithium is a natural substance found in small amounts in certain soils and mineral springs. It curbs mania, eases sadness and helps prevent your mood from changing from one extreme to another. Lithium has been used in the United States to treat bipolar disorder since 1974. How it works remains a mystery, but it improves symptoms in about 60 percent to 80 percent of people with the illness.

Lithium is sold under the brand names Eskalith and Lithobid, and as the generic drug lithium carbonate. If you take this medication, your doctor will need to measure lithium levels in your blood to adjust the dose to the correct amount. Certain medications can increase lithium levels in the bloodstream. They include non-steroidal anti-inflammatory drugs (NSAIDs), such as ibuprofen (Advil, Motrin, Nuprin), ketoprofen (Actron, Orudis) and naproxen (Aleve). Some high blood pressure medications, including hydro-chlorothiazide (HydroDiuril, Microzide) and angiotensin-convert-ing enzyme (ACE) inhibitors (Accupril, Lotensin, Vasotec) also can affect lithium levels. Always check with your doctor about possible drug interactions when adding a new medication or using over-the-counter pain preparations.

The most common side effects of lithium are nausea, diarrhea, fatigue, confusion and trembling hands. Occasionally, it also causes thirst and excessive urination. Some of these symptoms fade in a few days, but thirst, excessive urination and trembling hands may persist. Contact your doctor if you experience these symptoms.

**Anticonvulsants.** Valproic acid (Depakote) and carbamazepine (Carbatrol, Tegretol) are anticonvulsant drugs prescribed primarily for seizure disorders (epilepsy). They also treat bipolar disorder.

Valproic acid or carbamazepine may be effective even in cir-cumstances where lithium fails, such as in rapid-cycling bipolar

## Lithium augmentation

Sometimes doctors will prescribe lithium to depressed people who don't have bipolar disorder. This usually happens when an antidepressant alone isn't working. When taken with an antidepressant, lithium can strengthen the effect of the antidepressant or help it to work. This combined approach is called lithium augmentation.

disorder. People with this form of the disorder experience four or more mood episodes annually. In some instances, valproic acid or carbamazepine are taken in combination with lithium. It's uncertain exactly how anticonvulsants help bipolar disorder.

Like other medications, anticonvulsants produce side effects. Valproic acid may cause sedation, increased appetite, weight gain and digestive problems. Taking the medication with food can help reduce digestive troubles. Side effects of carbamazepine include drowsiness, dizziness, confusion, headaches and nausea. One of the most common side effects, a skin rash, often goes away if you stop taking the drug. The medications can also cause liver problems in some people. Before you take either drug, your doctor will likely test your liver to make sure that you don't have any liver problems and that it's safe for you to take the drug. Another potentially serious side effect of carbamazepine is that it can lower your white blood cell count. Most often, the reduction is minor, but sometimes it can be severe, increasing your risk of infection.

Newer anticonvulsant medications being studied for treatment of bipolar depression include gabapentin (Neurontin) and lamotrigine (Lamictal).

### Anti-anxiety medications

Depression and anxiety often occur together. Antidepressants — especially SSRIs or mirtazapine — often control anxiety as well as treat depression. But because antidepressants can take several weeks to start working, your doctor may prescribe a second medication for a short time to help control anxiety until the antidepressant becomes effective. You may also be given another medication if an antidepressant alone isn't effective.

Sedatives called benzodiazepines work quickly — often within 30 to 90 minutes — to ease anxiety. But these drugs have two major drawbacks: They can become habit forming if taken for more than a few weeks, and they aren't effective at controlling depression. For these reasons, doctors usually prescribe them for only a short time to help you get over a particularly anxious period or until the antidepressant has time to become effective. The most commonly prescribed sedatives to control anxiety include:

- Alprazolam (Xanax)
- Chlordiazepoxide (Librium)
- Clonazepam (Klonopin)
- Diazepam (Valium)
- Lorazepam (Ativan)

Sedatives may cause dizziness, drowsiness, imbalance and reduced muscle coordination. Higher doses and long-term use can interfere with memory. It's important when discontinuing sedatives to reduce the dose gradually over several days or weeks, working with your doctor. This can help prevent withdrawal symptoms, such as nausea, loss of appetite, irritability, insomnia, headache, dizziness and trembling.

For more severe anxiety, your doctor may recommend the medication buspirone (BuSpar). It's often effective in treating anxiety that's not helped by antidepressants. Buspirone can also be effective for generalized anxiety disorder, a condition in which you worry excessively or worry for no apparent reason. The medication influences the activity of serotonin but in a different way than SSRIs. Like antidepressants, it may take 2 to 3 weeks for buspirone to become effective, and it can take up to 6 weeks before you experience the drug's full effect. Unfortunately, buspirone often doesn't work as well if you've taken benzodiazepines in the past.

Common side effects of buspirone include a feeling of lightheadedness shortly after taking the medicine. This usually lasts just a few minutes. Less common side effects include headaches, nausea, nervousness and insomnia.

### Antipsychotic medications
Available since the 1950s, antipsychotic medications are typically

prescribed for severe cases of depression accompanied by psychosis, a condition in which people experience hallucinations or delusions. Some of the more commonly used antipsychotic medications include:

- Haloperidol (Haldol)
- Olanzapine (Zyprexa)
- Quetiapine (Seroquel)
- Risperidone (Risperdal)
- Thioridazine (Mellaril)
- Trifluoperazine (Stelazine)
- Ziprasidone (Geodon)

Antipsychotics block the effects of the neurotransmitter dopamine, associated with psychosis. The medications are often effective, but they can cause side effects in some people, including weight gain, dry mouth, blurred vision, constipation, drowsiness and increased tendency to sunburn. Occasionally, antipsychotics produce involuntary contractions of small muscles in your face, lips, tongue and, sometimes, other body parts. This is more common with older antipsychotics and with longer use of the drugs.

## New medications under study

Pharmaceutical companies continue to investigate new medications for treating depression, hoping to help people who don't benefit from current antidepressants or who find the side effects of current drugs intolerable. If research is successful, these medications may launch new classes of antidepressants, provide more treatment options and improve our understanding of depression's biology. Two types of medications being studied include:

**Substance P blocker.** This drug appears to block nerve cells from receiving messages from a nerve chemical called substance P. Substance P is found throughout your brain and spinal cord (central nervous system) and is involved with the transmission of pain signals. While researchers were studying the drug as a potential treatment for pain, they discovered that it had an antidepressant-like effect in some people who took it.

**CRF blocker.** An excessive amount of the hormone called corticotropin-releasing factor (CRF) may play a role in depression. Researchers speculate that CRF hormones, which can be activated by stress, stimulate the release of other chemicals in your brain that cause depression. Clinical studies involving animals and humans suggest that medications that block CRF from working on brain cells may reduce symptoms of depression.

Many studies are still necessary to determine if these two types of drugs are safe and effective and whether they interact with other medications. Researchers are especially eager to learn if these medications may be effective in people who haven't benefited from other antidepressants. Even if studies continue to show benefits, it will likely be several years before these medications are available.

## Herbal and dietary supplements

According to a recent study, more than one-third of people with severe depression or anxiety use some form of complementary or alternative therapy to treat their illness. This includes herbal and dietary supplements sold without a prescription. Due to their increasing popularity, some supplements are under critical review to determine their role in helping depression. Within several years, more will be known about these products, including their effectiveness, safety and how they interact with prescription medications.

Until then, talk with your doctor before taking any herbal or dietary supplement. Because alternative products aren't subject to the same pre-market regulations for safety and effectiveness as prescription medications, you can't be certain that such a product is free from contamination during its preparation or manufacture. Nor can you be confident the same product from different manufacturers is of equal quality and has consistent amounts of active ingredient. Even separate batches of product from the same manufacturer may be of different quality.

The pages that follow include some of the more popular supplements marketed or taken for treatment of depression.

## St. John's wort

St. John's wort is an herbal preparation from the *Hypericum perfora-tum* plant. It has long been used in folk medicine, and today it's widely used in Europe to treat anxiety, depression and sleep disorders. In the United States it's sold in health food stores and pharmacies in the form of tablets or a tea.

Some studies suggest St. John's wort may work as well as an antidepressant for mild to moderate depression, and with fewer side effects. But according to a large clinical trial published in the *Journal of the American Medical Association* in April 2001, it's ineffective for treatment of major depression. Results of another study on St. John's wort sponsored by the National Institutes of Health should be available in the near future.

Adverse reactions to this herbal preparation can include dry mouth, dizziness, digestive problems, fatigue, confusion and sensitivity to sunlight. In most cases, reactions are mild. One important concern is that St. John's wort can interfere with the effectiveness of certain prescription medications, including antidepressants, drugs to treat human immunodeficiency virus (HIV) and AIDS, and drugs taken to prevent organ rejection in people who've had transplants. It can also increase the risk of serotonin syndrome if it's taken with an SSRI or another serotonin-active antidepressant.

## SAM-e

The term *SAM-e* (pronounced sammy) is short for S-adenosyl-methionine, a chemical substance used in Europe to treat depression. It's available there as a prescription drug. In the United States it's sold as an over-the-counter supplement. SAM-e is found in human cells and plays a role in many body functions. It's thought to increase levels of serotonin and dopamine, though this still needs to be confirmed in larger studies. European studies suggest it works as well as standard antidepressants but with milder side effects.

SAM-e pills are expensive, especially considering their unproven effectiveness. *Consumer Reports* recently compared a dozen brands and found that the price for a daily dose ranges from $1.80 to $8.75. The magazine also found the amount of S-adenosyl-methionine in tablets varied. Too much of the product can be harmful.

## Omega-3 fatty acids

Omega-3 fatty acids are found in fish oils and certain plants. They're being investigated as a possible mood stabilizer for people with bipolar disorder. Some studies suggest that people with depression have decreased amounts of an active ingredient found in omega-3 fatty acids. One small study suggests that omega-3 fatty acids may prevent relapse among people with bipolar disorder.

Fish oil capsules containing omega-3 fatty acids are sold in stores. The capsules are high in fat and calories and may produce gastrointestinal problems. Another way to get more omega-3s is simply to eat more cold-water fish, such as salmon, mackerel and herring.

## 5-HTP

One of the raw materials that your body needs to make serotonin is a chemical called 5-hydroxytryptophan (5-HTP). This product is prescribed in Europe to treat depression. In the United States it's available as an over-the-counter supplement.

In theory, if you boost your body's level of 5-HTP, you should also elevate serotonin levels. A small study compared 5-HTP with the SSRI fluvoxamine. People taking three daily doses of 100 milligrams of 5-HTP reported slightly more relief than those taking fluvoxamine, and with fewer side effects. But there's not enough evidence to determine if 5-HTP is effective and safe. Larger studies are needed.

### Americans favor more regulations

Recent polls show that when it comes to alternative products, Americans favor greater government control. The Harvard School of Public Health conducted national opinion polls and found that the majority of people polled support regulations that would give the Food and Drug Administration authority to review dietary supplements for safety before their sale and to remove from stores products that are unsafe. Survey respondents also stated that they would like to see increased government regulation regarding the advertising of dietary supplements to help ensure that claims about the products are true.

In the 1980s a serious medical complication developed in some people who took 5-HTP from a bad batch. Many suffered permanent neurological damage and several died. This is an example of why you should be cautious when considering use of unregulated herbal and dietary supplements.

## Chapter 8

# *Counseling and psychotherapy*

L ong before medical treatments were developed for depression, people found comfort and relief from emotional distress by "unburdening the soul" — discussing their problems and fears. During difficult times, it's natural to turn to a friend, a family member, a doctor or a member of the clergy. Talking with someone you trust in order to relieve distress and receive advice remains an integral part of depression treatment. Today, these discussions often take place with a licensed mental health professional.

The terms *counseling* and *psychotherapy* are most often used to describe this component of treatment. They're not specific terms for a certain kind of treatment. Rather, they refer to receiving help from a mental health professional by some combination of talking and listening. *Talk therapy* is another common term for this practice. Just as there are different types of medications, so too there are different types of counseling and psychotherapy.

## Counseling

*Counseling* is a general term for advice given by a professional. You may seek counseling for information and advice about many types of concerns — legal, financial, career or spiritual. People who are

## Counseling in action

Janet, who's in her mid-30s, visits her family doctor because she's not sleeping well, has lost her appetite, has an upset stomach and has been feeling very tired. Her doctor completes a medical evaluation and finds her physical health to be good. Janet's doctor thinks depression is the likely problem and wants to learn more about Janet.

Janet has a deep religious faith. She met, fell in love with and married her husband within the church. They've been raising their two children within a strong faith. Recently, though, Janet's husband informed her that he has lost his faith. Janet is devastated. Embarrassed and uncertain, she feels alone and doesn't know what to do. Janet tells her doctor that in addition to her physical problems, for the last couple of months, she has felt sad, has withdrawn from many activities that she used to enjoy and often finds herself crying.

Janet's doctor tells her that her symptoms are most likely related to depression and that her depression is probably linked to stress. Her doctor suggests that she meet with her pastor for counseling and asks Janet to come back in several weeks so that they can discuss how she's doing.

Janet finds that after several counseling sessions with her pastor, in which she learns that all is not lost and that her church will continue to be supportive, she starts to feel better and her symptoms begin to disappear.

depressed often seek counseling from various professionals: a doctor, a mental health professional or a member of the clergy. Much of the information in this book, if provided to you by a professional, could be considered counseling.

Although the terms *counseling* and *psychotherapy* are often used interchangeably, the term *psychotherapy* denotes a process of receiving help from a mental health professional that's more involved and more individualized than the general information and advice associated with counseling.

# Psychotherapy

*Psychotherapy* can be an unclear and often confusing term. One reason for the confusion is that there are many different types of psychotherapy. Another reason is that some people view psychotherapy as psychoanalysis — an intense, prolonged and expensive form of treatment that's less frequently used today. Psychotherapy describes treatment for mental illness that involves listening, talking, dealing with thoughts and emotions, and changing behaviors.

Techniques of psychotherapy have evolved over time, and many advances have occurred that have made psychotherapy more accessible, affordable and effective, and less time-consuming.

In the pages that follow, we describe several forms of psychotherapy to treat depression. It can be confusing to read about the different forms and then attempt to equate what you've read with your own experience or that of a family member or a friend. That's because skilled therapists often tailor psychotherapy treatment to the specific needs of each individual. This may require combining elements from several different approaches into an integrated approach designed to best help the person who's depressed.

## Types of psychotherapy

With each type of psychotherapy, you work closely with a licensed mental health professional to treat your condition. But different forms of psychotherapy have different goals. Some forms are aimed at helping you to identify unhealthy thoughts and behaviors that are contributing to your depression and to replace them with healthier ones. Some are designed to help you cope with an immediate crisis, such as the death of a loved one, a troubled marriage or a financial crisis. Other forms are designed to explore underlying stress, anxieties or problematic patterns of behavior that may be triggering depression.

Studies suggest that for treating depression, a short-term, goal-oriented approach often is the most successful. Two forms of psychotherapy that have proved very effective are cognitive behavior therapy and interpersonal therapy.

### Selecting a therapist

Anyone can set up shop as a "psychotherapist." Therefore, you want to make sure the person you select to help you is a licensed mental health professional. The four major groups of mental health professionals are:

- Psychiatrists
- Psychologists
- Psychiatric nurses
- Social workers

These professionals are licensed by state boards and must update their knowledge and skills with continuing education. (For more information on the types of mental health professionals, see Chapter 4.)

It's also important that you feel comfortable with your therapist and confident in his or her skills, since you may be confiding intimate thoughts, feelings and fears to this person. The National Mental Health Association advises that you avoid individuals or organizations that:

- Don't answer questions to your satisfaction
- Promise financial rewards if you make an appointment or participate in a program
- Offer or imply a guarantee of success
- Try to involve you in a long-term financial commitment

During your introductory meeting with a therapist, don't hesitate to talk about fees, length of therapy, insurance coverage and other practical matters. Keep in mind that some health care plans limit your choice of mental health care providers. Your insurance plan may require you to see a family doctor first or to choose a mental health professional from within a specific network.

## Cognitive behavior therapy

Cognitive behavior therapy (CBT) is based on the foundation that "you are what you think." Or rather, how you feel is a result of how you think about yourself and your life circumstances. This type of therapy proposes that pessimistic thoughts and negative views of life events contribute to depression. According to this theory, people experiencing depression often have:

- A negative view of themselves, seeing themselves as worthless, inadequate, helpless, unlovable and deficient
- A negative view of their environment, seeing it as overwhelming, unsupportive and filled with obstacles
- A negative view of the future, seeing it as hopeless

## Making unhealthy assumptions

Are you prone to pessimism or negative thoughts? Persistent negative assumptions can contribute to depression. The first step to changing unhealthy thinking patterns is to recognize them. Negative, irrational thinking patterns may include the following:

**Catastrophizing.** You automatically anticipate the worst: "I got a message to call my boss. I bet I'm getting fired."

**Overgeneralizing.** You see a troubling event as the beginning of an unending cycle: "I have a headache this morning. I probably won't be able to go for my walk today. That means I'll gain weight. It's going to be a terrible week."

**Personalizing.** You interpret events that have nothing to do with you as a reflection on you: "One person left the gathering early. She must have found me boring."

**All-or-nothing thinking.** You see things only in extremes, as black or white. There's no middle ground: "If I don't score 100 percent on the exam, I'm a failure."

**Emotionalizing.** You allow your feelings to control your judgment: "I feel stupid and boring, so I must be stupid and boring."

**Filtering.** You magnify the negative aspects of a situation and filter out all of the positive ones: "I'm being promoted. I won't have to work weekends and I suppose the pay will be better. But what if I have to move to a new department? What if I don't get along with the people there? What if I have to learn a new computer program?"

## Who can benefit?

The goal of cognitive behavior therapy is to replace negative thoughts with more positive, realistic perceptions. You do this by learning to recognize depressive reactions and associated thoughts

## Cognitive behavior therapy in action

Things were going well for Tom until his company announced it would be laying off 10 percent of the workforce in the next few months. Everyone is nervous. No one knows who will get cut. Tom has performed well, but has never felt confident in his job skills. He thinks he's sure to be laid off.

The stress is getting to Tom. He wakes up in the middle of the night and can't fall back to sleep. He loses his appetite. He feels hopeless and helpless about the future. His family doctor refers him to a psychologist to help him manage his depression and anxiety. "What can I do?" he asks the therapist. "This job is all I know how to do. No one else needs me. And they don't want someone my age. Now my kids won't be able to go to college, and we're going to lose our house and the car."

"Not so fast," the psychologist tells him. "These are real concerns, but you've already lost your house and car before you even know if you're going to lose your job."

Through cognitive behavior therapy, Tom identifies his automatic negative thoughts and begins to identify and then use more positive ways of assessing the situation.

as they occur, usually by keeping a journal of your thoughts and responses. You and your therapist then develop ways to challenge these negative reactions and thoughts. This may include homework assignments, such as reading about depression or communicating with others. These assignments help you learn how to replace negative responses with more positive ones. Eventually, the process becomes automatic.

Cognitive behavior therapy is a short-term treatment that usually includes between 12 and 16 therapy sessions. This form of therapy has been well researched, and studies show it works particularly well in treating mild to moderate depression. A large study by the National Institute of Mental Health compared three different treatments for depression and found cognitive behavior therapy was effective for mild depression but not as effective as medication for severe depression. Research also suggests that there's less risk of future depressive episodes with cognitive behavior therapy than with medications. A combination of therapy and medication is often more effective than either alone.

## Interpersonal therapy

Interpersonal therapy (IPT) focuses on relationships as the key to understanding and overcoming signs and symptoms associated with depression. The goal of interpersonal therapy is to improve your relationship and communication skills and boost your self-esteem. Interpersonal therapy typically explores four areas:

- Unresolved grief
- Conflicts or disputes with others
- Transitions from one social or occupational role to another
- Difficulties with interpersonal or people skills

Like cognitive behavior therapy, interpersonal therapy is short term, generally involving 12 to 16 treatment sessions. Interpersonal therapy has three phases of treatment. The initial phase focuses on identifying problem areas, the middle phase focuses on dealing with and resolving one or more key issues, and the last phase focuses on ending the therapy.

### Interpersonal therapy in action

Kate has moved away from home, where she was close to her family and a few good friends, to attend school in a city where she doesn't know anyone. She doesn't have much confidence in her ability to make new friends, and her early efforts at making new friendships have failed. She is feeling alone and isolated and is having trouble adjusting. She has several symptoms of depression: easy tearfulness, disrupted sleep, poor appetite, an uncharacteristic tendency to hole up in her room. Plus, she isn't finding much pleasure in activities she once enjoyed.

Kate sees a psychologist at the university's mental health center. The psychologist uses interpersonal therapy to help Kate navigate this transition and build relationship skills and self-confidence. Over several weeks, Kate's symptoms begin to diminish.

## Who can benefit?

Interpersonal therapy can be effective in reducing symptoms of mild to moderate depression and in improving your ability to form relationships and function in social settings. In a comparison of interpersonal therapy and antidepressant drug treatment, the two were equally effective, although medication worked faster. A combination of therapy and medication is often more effective than either alone. The comparison study found that a year after treatment, people who received interpersonal therapy and medication were functioning better than those who received only medication.

## Other forms of psychotherapy

Many people who are depressed benefit the most from individual sessions with their therapist. But some find a group setting more beneficial. Others find it helpful to attend therapy sessions with their spouse, partner or family. Group, couples or family therapy may be based on cognitive behavior strategies, interpersonal techniques or a combination of these or other therapies.

### Group therapy

Group therapy involves a group of unrelated people and one or more mental health professionals who help facilitate the therapy. It isn't the same as a support group, which may be led by peers or laypersons rather than professionals. Group therapy strives toward many of the same goals as individual therapy, but relies on advice, feedback and support from others in the group on how to deal with and change troubling problems.

Some groups are designed for people with common issues, such as depression, domestic violence, substance abuse or compulsive gambling. Other groups are more general. Either way, both the therapist and the group members play a crucial role in helping people move beyond conflict to insight. Often a group member discovers that his or her past experience is helpful to another member.

Group sessions can take place in a private practice, community mental health center, hospital or other professional setting. People who generally benefit most from group therapy are individuals who are willing to share personal experiences, thoughts and feelings with a group, and who are willing to hear about other people's fears and frustrations, instead of focusing solely on their own problems.

### Couples and family therapy

Couples and family therapy can be useful in helping spouses, partners and families work together to overcome depression and other mental illnesses that may be associated with depression. Instead of focusing on the individual, couples and family therapy focuses on the unit — the interaction between the couple or family members.

A couple or family may decide to seek therapy together if they're having serious problems that interfere with their normal functioning or if individual therapy doesn't seem to be helping. Common issues among couples that may be helped by therapy include communication difficulties, sexual problems and differing expectations of the relationship. The goal is to resolve the problems as quickly and effectively as possible. Among couples who receive counseling, about two-thirds improve.

## How long does psychotherapy last?

Depending on how severe your depression is and the type of therapy you choose, psychotherapy may last just a few sessions or continue for several months. In general, the more severe or complicated the depression, the longer the time needed to treat it.

For most people, short-term therapy is effective in treating mild to moderate depression. In a major national study, half of the people studied showed significant improvement after eight therapy sessions, and three-fourths improved after 6 months. Sometimes even a single therapy session can provide the reassurance, confidence or insight needed to overcome depression. Once your therapy sessions are over, your doctor or therapist may request that you return for periodic checkups to discuss how you're doing.

Long-term therapy — sometimes called insight-oriented therapy, psychodynamic therapy or supportive therapy — generally lasts more than 6 months and may continue for several years. The goal of this type of therapy is less to treat depression and more to identify and change patterns of behavior that increase a person's risk of depression. For example, a young man, who is now improved following treatment for his third bout of depression in 5 years, has linked the onset of each of his depressive episodes to relationships that have ended badly when he wasn't able to make a serious commitment. Through long-term therapy he hopes to better understand why he has trouble committing to a relationship to prevent the pattern from continuing.

Individuals most likely to benefit from long-term therapy are those whose depression is accompanied by another mental illness, such as an anxiety disorder, an eating disorder, substance abuse, a personality disorder, or by persistently painful or costly patterns of behavior.

## How does psychotherapy work?

Over the long term, psychotherapy can provide many benefits and play an important role in the treatment of mild to moderate depression. It can help you understand yourself better, equip you with problem-solving skills, provide you with more effective ways of dealing with life events and help you address and express powerful emotions. Psychotherapy can also be an effective treatment for some people with mild to moderate depression who don't want to take antidepressant medication or who can't tolerate its side effects. Many times, medication and psychotherapy are combined.

Exactly how psychotherapy improves depression isn't known. That's partly because different types of psychotherapy work in different manners. Mental health professionals believe psychotherapy influences depression in the following ways:

- Learning about depression and what you can do to treat it gives you a feeling of reassurance. By actively working with a mental health professional to manage your depression, you also gain a sense of mastery — belief that you're in control and that you can get better.

- Changing negative thoughts, attitudes, behaviors and relationships to more healthy, positive ones can go a long way toward reducing stress or better managing stress. These positive changes may also result in improved relationships with others, as well as a more comfortable relationship with yourself.
- Expressing your feelings in a supportive, therapeutic relationship can be beneficial. Some label this as venting. Discussing emotional material in the proper setting can also promote insight, release negative emotions and promote change.
- Brain imaging research shows that cognitive behavior therapy can produce changes in brain activity in regions associated with depression. It's not known if these changes reflect the effects of stress reduction or improved stress management, or if they're a direct result of the therapy. But the studies strongly support the close link between state of mind and brain activity.

### Feeling 'stuck'

During the course of psychotherapy, you may wonder if the treatment is helping you. Keep in mind that having negative feelings about psychotherapy doesn't mean it's not working. Confronting difficult issues can be scary and overwhelming. Some resistance or anger is a normal part of the process.

If you're concerned about a certain aspect of your therapy, talk to your therapist about it. Maybe you get the feeling that your therapist doesn't understand your fears or frustrations. Maybe you have difficulty communicating with your therapist. Or maybe you're uneasy with your therapist's body language or behavior. These all are important issues worth discussing.

If you're not satisfied with the answer you receive, you continue to feel uneasy or you're not showing signs of improvement after a period of weeks to several months, you may want to get a second opinion.

## Making it work

Psychotherapy can be successful only when both you and your therapist are dedicated to achieving a successful outcome. The therapist's skills are important, but what you bring to the table matters too — your attitude, expectations and commitment. If you go into therapy with the attitude that "no one can really help me" or "this will never work," the chances of success are greatly reduced.

It's important during therapy sessions to be honest, face up to some possibly painful truths, deal with uncomfortable feelings, and be open to new insights and ways of doing things. In turn, the therapist will listen carefully, clarify, interpret and help guide you toward more healthy behaviors. The process involves mutual trust, respect and confidentiality.

## Chapter 9

# Electroconvulsive and other biomedical therapies

Sometimes antidepressant medications and psychotherapy aren't effective. Or based on a person's health status, they may not be appropriate. Fortunately, other options are available. This chapter looks at two other forms of treatment for depression: electroconvulsive therapy (ECT) and light therapy. You'll also read about possible future therapies under study.

## Electroconvulsive therapy

For many people, electroconvulsive therapy conjures up images from the novel and movie *One Flew Over the Cuckoo's Nest*. But that movie and others like it are outdated and inaccurate portrayals of this method of treating depression. Study after study indicates that ECT is a safe, effective and efficient treatment. Still it remains mired in controversy because of its early history of misuse and sometimes negative portrayals in the media. The truth is, ECT is one of the most dramatically effective treatments for severe depression that modern medicine has to offer.

### Some history
The origins of ECT date back to the early 1930s when scientists felt

that they could treat mental illnesses by inducing seizures. To treat depression and other mental disorders, researchers injected individuals with chemical substances that caused a seizure. The practice was highly effective in some people, but many found the seizures terrifying. The use of chemicals also proved unreliable.

An important advance occurred in April 1938 when two Italian researchers used electrical current instead of a chemical substance to induce a seizure in a mentally ill person. A man experiencing delusions and hallucinations experienced a full recovery after 11 ECT treatments. This success prompted the rapid spread of ECT as a treatment for mental illness, including depression.

Misperceptions regarding ECT — that it's painful and downright dangerous — stem from accounts of its early use. Doctors first began using ECT in the United States in 1940. Back then the therapy was delivered without anesthesia or muscle relaxants. You were fully awake, and hospital staff was close by to hold your shoulders, arms, and legs before and during the seizure. What's more, doctors used a much stronger electrical current to trigger the seizure than they do today. As a result, side effects and complications of the procedure sometimes were significant.

### How ECT works

Today, ECT is a scientifically refined treatment that's increasingly being performed on an outpatient basis and in a setting resembling that used for minor surgical procedures. The total time under anesthesia is about 10 minutes, with an additional 30 to 45 minutes in the recovery room. The treatment team usually includes a psychiatrist, a nurse and an anesthesiologist or a nurse anesthetist.

Typical of many large medical centers, Mayo Clinic performs ECT as follows: Before the procedure, you're examined and asked a series of questions to make sure you're prepared for the treatment. You're then wheeled into the room where the procedure is performed. While you're lying down, the doctor places small electrodes, each about the size of a silver dollar, on your head.

While the electrodes are being positioned, you're given intravenous injections of a short-acting anesthetic to make you go to sleep and a muscle relaxant to prevent shaking that can occur during the seizure. As the anesthetic begins to take effect, an oxygen mask is placed over your mouth to help you breathe. Other medications may be given intravenously, depending on other health conditions you may have. Blood pressure cuffs are placed around an arm and an ankle.

When you're asleep from the anesthesia and your muscles are relaxed, the doctor presses a button on the ECT machine. This causes a small amount of electrical current to pass through the electrodes to your brain, producing a seizure that usually lasts 30 to 60 seconds. Because of the anesthesia and muscle relaxant, you remain relaxed and unaware of the seizure. The only outward indication that you're experiencing a seizure may be a rhythmic movement of a foot or a hand. When a blood pressure cuff is placed around an ankle or a forearm and inflated, it prevents the muscle relaxant from temporarily paralyzing muscles in the corresponding foot or hand. The foot or hand shakes during a seizure, helping to confirm that a seizure has occurred.

During the seizure your heart rate, blood pressure and oxygen use are carefully monitored. An electroencephalogram (EEG) records your brain activity, in much the same way as an electrocardiogram (ECG) measures your heart activity. Sudden, increased activity signals the beginning of a seizure and the leveling off of your EEG tracing indicates when the seizure is over. A few minutes later, the effects of the anesthesia and the muscle relaxant begin to wear off, and you're moved to a recovery area where a nurse monitors you. Upon awakening you may experience a period of confusion lasting from a few minutes to a few hours or more.

### ECT and brain function

No one knows for certain how ECT helps treat depression. It is known, though, that many chemical aspects of brain functioning are altered during and after seizure activity. Researchers theorize that when ECT is administered on a regular basis, these chemical changes build upon one another, somehow reducing depression.

Most people who receive ECT have 6 to 12 treatments over several weeks. Usually, you receive a treatment two to three times a week. Once your symptoms improve, you'll need some form of

## ECT: A look inside

A session of electroconvulsive therapy (ECT) generally takes between 1 and 2 hours from the time you arrive for the procedure until you go home or return to your hospital room. To help you visualize how the treatment works, here are pictures of a person receiving ECT at Mayo Clinic.

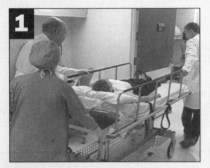

After meeting with health care staff, who make sure that you're ready for treatment, you lie down on a gurney and are wheeled into the room where the procedure is performed.

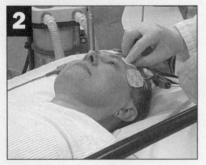

Once in the room, a doctor places small pads with attached wires (electrodes) on your scalp. The electrodes are connected to the ECT machine. The doctor also places other pads on your scalp that monitor your brain activity.

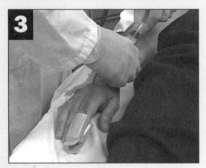

You're given two types of medication — an anesthetic and a muscle relaxant — through an intravenous (IV) line located in your lower arm.

When the electrodes are in place and the medications have taken effect, a doctor presses a button on the ECT machine, causing a small, precise amount of electrical current to pass from the machine through the electrodes and to your brain.

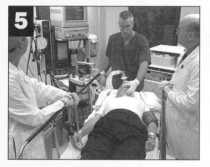

The electrical current causes a brain seizure that generally lasts from 30 to 60 seconds. During the seizure, medical personnel monitor your vital signs.

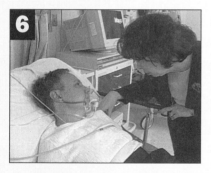

Once the seizure has ended, the procedure is over. The pads are removed, and you're wheeled into a recovery area where a nurse looks after you until you awake.

When you're feeling well enough, a family member or friend can take you home or you may return to your hospital room. A nurse discusses precautions you should take until the effects of the medications have worn off.

ongoing treatment to prevent a relapse into depression. You may receive an antidepressant after your ECT treatments, or you may continue to receive ECT on a less frequent basis, called maintenance or continuation ECT. With maintenance ECT, your sessions may be reduced to once a week, then every other week and gradually taper to once a month or so for several months. Some people receive periodic ECT treatments for a year or more.

ECT is effective in approximately 80 percent of the people who complete the course of treatment. Its effects often aren't immediate, but ECT generally works more quickly than medication. Many people begin to notice an improvement in their symptoms after two or three treatments and are generally pleased with the results.

### Are you a candidate?

Your doctor may recommend ECT to treat your depression if you:

**Need treatment to rapidly address serious symptoms.** Perhaps your symptoms are severe enough that you or your doctor worry that you may attempt suicide. In some cases of severe depression, people refuse food and fluids to the point where their physical health is greatly at risk. Occasionally, individuals with severe depression experience delusions or hallucinations that cause great distress and put them at risk of hurting themselves or someone

---

**'It's working quite well'**

*The treatments that they were using to treat my depression weren't working — namely the medications and the therapy. So it was recommended that I use ECT. They started out by giving me treatments once every other day. So I was getting three treatments a week: Monday, Wednesday and Friday. I wasn't feeling much better initially. Then — probably after the first week, week and a half — I began to experience a nice recovery. The first thing I noticed was that I started sleeping through the night again, which was nice because I had such disrupted sleep when I was depressed. Then I started getting my energy back and that type of thing. I've been on a maintenance level of treatment for ECT, so I get a treatment every other Friday and it's working quite well.*

Joanne
Rochester, Minnesota

else. In these situations, you don't have time to wait for antidepressants to take effect.

**Don't improve with other treatments.** When you've tried psychotherapy and at least two antidepressants to no avail, ECT is often your next best bet.

**Can't tolerate the side effects of antidepressant medications.** Some people are extremely sensitive to antidepressants and experience significant side effects from even the lowest possible doses.

**Didn't respond well to other treatments during previous depression.** There may be little point in pursuing treatment that you already know doesn't work.

**Have had success with ECT in the past.** It makes sense to stay with what works.

### Before your treatment

As with any procedure in which anesthesia is used, before your first treatment, you'll need a medical evaluation to make sure you don't have a health problem that may prevent you from receiving anesthesia or the treatment. An evaluation usually includes:

- A medical history
- A physical examination
- Basic blood tests
- An ECG to check for heart disease

Before you receive ECT you'll need to give your informed consent. Informed consent means that you've been told about and understand the benefits and risks of the procedure, and that you give health care staff permission to perform the procedure on you. You can withdraw your consent at any stage of treatment. If you aren't capable of providing consent, your doctor must follow state and local laws that indicate under what circumstances you can receive ECT. Some form of substituted consent, often from a family member or a legally appointed guardian, must be obtained. However, regulations vary quite a bit from state to state.

### The pros and cons

The main benefit of ECT is that it's often effective for depression when other treatments aren't helpful. It also tends to work more quickly than medication or psychotherapy. However, ECT can cause side effects. The main side effects are:

**Memory impairment.** Immediately following an ECT treatment, you may experience a period of confusion. You may not know where you are or why you're there. This generally lasts from a few minutes to several hours and often gets longer with each succeeding treatment. Occasionally, the confusion may last several days. After the course of treatment is over, the confusion clears up.

New memories that are formed during your course of treatment also may be lost. For example, you may have trouble remembering conversations with others during this period. This type of memory loss also should clear up after the treatments are stopped.

The final type of memory impairment caused by ECT relates to long-term memory. Most often ECT affects memories that are formed just before or during your course of treatment. In some rare instances, though, people have trouble remembering life events going back several years. Sometimes these long-term memories come back after the ECT treatments are done. Other times they remain permanently forgotten.

### 'I consider it kind of a balance'

*During the treatments, I never forgot who I was, where I lived, how old I was, my children — any of those kinds of things. I never forgot what kinds of things I did at work. The memory loss has to do more with incidents of not remembering trips that we might have taken. For example, one of my children might call me up and say, Do you remember when we came to visit over Easter? and I have no recall of that.*

*When I get depressed I'm unable to function and work. I'm unable to enjoy life. It robs me of my being. ECT treatment gives that back to me because I'm healthy and well. I do have what I would consider a minor effect — which is the memory problem — especially with the maintenance treatment. And that's worth it as far as I'm concerned. I consider it kind of a balance. If I balance out the two sides, I'd take the memory loss side effect any day because I'm well and can function again, and I have my life back.*

Joanne

Rochester, Minnesota

**Medical complications.** As with any type of medical procedure, especially one in which anesthesia is used, there are risks of medical complications. The pre-ECT medical evaluation helps identify medical conditions that may put you at increased risk of complications, enabling your doctors to take special precautions that lessen such risks.

**Bodily discomforts.** On the days you have an ECT treatment, you may experience nausea, headache, muscle ache or jaw pain. These are common and can easily be treated with medications. They may be distressing, but they're not serious.

**Relapse.** Without some form of ongoing treatment after a successful course of ECT treatment, about 90 percent of people have a relapse of depression within a year. To reduce your risk of relapse, it's important to receive ongoing treatment with an antidepressant or maintenance ECT.

## Light therapy

People with seasonal affective disorder (SAD) typically experience depression during the darkest time of the year, when sunlight is limited. Symptoms may include feelings of sadness, loss of energy and sleep difficulties. As the days gradually get longer and sunlight becomes more bountiful, these symptoms disappear. A common treatment for this type of depression is light therapy, also called phototherapy. Light therapy has been used since the early 1980s, and it has many benefits. It's easy to administer, it usually doesn't have major side effects, and it's cost-effective.

### Lighting up

Light therapy consists of exposure to intense light under specified conditions. The lighting system most often used with light therapy is a box that you set on a table or a desktop. The box contains a set of fluorescent bulbs with a diffusing screen. The screen helps block out ultraviolet rays, which can cause cataracts and skin problems.

Treatment involves sitting close to the light box with the lights on and your eyes open. You shouldn't look directly at the light, but you want your head and body oriented so that the light can enter your eyes. You sit near the light box for 15 minutes to 2 hours once a day, generally in the morning. Studies comparing the use of light therapy in the morning with light therapy in the evening found that exposure to bright light in the morning is usually the most effective. But depending on your needs and the lighting system you have, your light treatment may be split into separate sessions. Many people read, write or have breakfast while undergoing light therapy.

Researchers believe that when bright light enters your eyes, it not only alerts the area of your brain that regulates your daily biological clock but also causes other positive psychological effects. Studies show that blood levels of the hormone melatonin are reduced when your eyes are exposed to bright light. Melatonin is produced during darkness and helps control your body's internal (circadian) rhythms of body temperature, hormone secretion and sleep. Depending on the time of day that you undergo light therapy, your body's internal clock either shifts ahead or is delayed.

Researchers also speculate that light therapy may have antidepressantlike effects in people with SAD, causing changes in neurotransmitter activity in certain brain areas. Scientists are studying the effects of bright light on production of the neurotransmitters serotonin and dopamine.

The idea of using light to treat depression stems from research on animal behavior and how it's affected by the seasons. Changes in sleep, eating and behavior patterns all seem to be finely tuned for each species to the length of day wherever they live.

**Phototherapy for SAD involves sitting near a bright light for a specified period each day. You shouldn't stare at the light, but you want the light to enter your eyes.**

### Not just any light

Simply sitting in front of a light in your home won't relieve symptoms of SAD. Indoor lights don't provide the type and intensity of light that's necessary to treat the condition. The specialized light boxes used in SAD give off light that's comparable to outdoor light just after sunrise or just before sunset — an intensity that's at least five times greater than ordinary indoor light. The recommended intensity level of light therapy for SAD is often between 2,500 and 10,000 lux (a measurement of light).

Light apparatuses used in light therapy are available commercially, but seek your doctor's opinion before purchasing such a unit, and use the apparatus only under your doctor's supervision to avoid complications. Light therapy needs to be monitored by a professional to achieve the best clinical outcome with the fewest side effects. It's also possible that the treatment may not work and symptoms of SAD may worsen.

### An effective treatment

Light therapy improves symptoms in about three out of four people with SAD. Many times people begin to feel better in just 4 or 5 days. Most people follow a consistent daily schedule of light therapy, beginning in the fall or winter in northern latitudes and continuing until spring when outdoor light alone is sufficient to maintain a good mood and high energy. If light treatment is interrupted during the winter months or it is stopped too soon, people with SAD often experience a return of depressive symptoms, often in less than a week.

Side effects are uncommon, and they're more likely to occur if you use light therapy in the evening. Some people experience irritability, eyestrain, headaches or insomnia. Usually these problems can be addressed by changing the time or duration of treatment.

In some instances, an antidepressant medication may be combined with light therapy. In cases where light therapy isn't effective, an antidepressant alone is often the next line of treatment. Antidepressants are also prescribed to people with SAD who don't want to reserve 15 minutes or more each day for light therapy. Antidepressants are generally effective, but they have the potential to cause more side effects.

# Possible future therapies: TMS and VNS

Researchers continue to study new treatments for depression. They're looking for treatments that may be more effective or cause fewer side effects than current methods. Following are two treatments being investigated.

### Transcranial magnetic stimulation

In some ways transcranial magnetic stimulation (TMS) is similar to electroconvulsive therapy. With TMS, electrical current passes through a wire coil located inside a hand-held device. The electrical current creates a strong magnetic pulse that passes through your scalp and skull when the device is held to your head. The magnetic pulse stimulates nerve cells located in the underlying brain.

The procedure usually takes about 20 to 30 minutes, during which time you're awake and alert. Unlike ECT, with TMS anesthesia isn't necessary, your brain doesn't receive direct electrical stimulation and the procedure doesn't intentionally cause a seizure. However, on occasion a seizure can occur. Another benefit of TMS is that it doesn't cause thinking or memory difficulties.

Most, but not all, studies indicate that magnetic brain stimulation once daily for 2 or more weeks may relieve depressive symptoms in people who haven't responded to other forms of treatment. TMS is still considered an experimental treatment, but evidence related to its safety and effectiveness has been favorable. TMS isn't recommended for people with implanted metal devices, such as a pacemaker, because the magnetic pulses may interfere with the devices' operation.

Many questions still need answers before TMS becomes an accepted and widely available treatment for depression. If

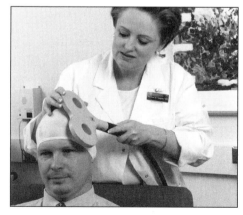

During transcranial magnetic stimulation, a device that emits a strong magnetic pulse is held to your scalp. The magnetic energy passes through your skull and stimulates nerve cells in your brain.

research produces successful results, it's possible that within 5 to 10 years TMS may be a common form of treatment for people with severe depression.

### Vagal nerve stimulation

The vagus nerve is an important nerve that connects your brainstem and organs in your chest and abdomen — your heart, lungs and intestines. The nerve runs from your abdomen and chest through your neck and into your brainstem through a tiny hole in your skull. It's an important route by which information travels to and from your central nervous system.

Vagal nerve stimulation (VNS) requires surgery during which a small electrical pulse generator about the size of a pocket watch — a pacemaker of sorts — is permanently placed in the upper-left side of your chest. Tiny wires are routed under your skin and up to your neck where they're wrapped around the vagus nerve. The generator is programmed to deliver tiny electrical pulses to the vagus nerve every few minutes.

Vagal nerve stimulation was originally developed to treat individuals with epilepsy who continued to have seizures despite use of medication. Researchers began to study its use in treating depression after they noted that people who received VNS to treat their seizure disorder experienced an improved mood. As with so many other treatments, no one knows for certain how vagal nerve stimulation improves depression.

In an initial study, 40 percent of people experiencing depression who received VNS improved. Further studies are under way to help determine the procedure's safety and effectiveness. Only after these studies are complete will doctors know if VNS holds promise as a treatment for depression.

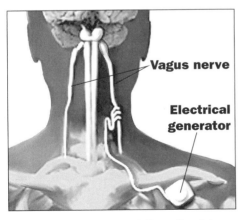

**A vagal nerve stimulator delivers tiny, intermittent electrical pulses to the vagus nerve. It's presently used to treat epilepsy and is being studied for treatment of depression.**

## What about acupuncture?

Acupuncture certainly isn't a new form of medical treatment. In fact, it's one of the oldest, first practiced by ancient Chinese healers. However, it's one of the few alternative methods of medical care to receive considerable study. Studies have compared acupuncture treatment with antidepressants and found acupuncture may be beneficial.

Acupuncture stems from the Chinese belief that below your skin are 14 invisible pathways, called meridians. Through these pathways flow Qi (chee), the Chinese word for life force. When the flow of Qi is interrupted, illness results. An acupuncturist applies pressure to specific points on your body to restore free flow of Qi and relieve symptoms. During a typical acupuncture session, the practitioner inserts hair-thin needles into your skin, which cause little or no pain. The needles remain in place for 15 to 40 minutes. Electrical stimulation also may be applied to the needles in a form of treatment called electroacupuncture.

In one study of 241 hospitalized patients with depression, researchers at Beijing Medical University in China divided the patients into two groups. One group received electroacupuncture, and the other received an antidepressant. Acupuncture worked as well as the drug and with fewer side effects.

Although acupuncture is gaining more acceptance as a legitimate treatment for some medical conditions, most doctors aren't ready yet to accept it as a primary treatment for depression.

## Chapter 10

# Self-help strategies

Professional treatment can bring your depression under control and help you feel better, but you still have to cope on a day-to-day basis. Life inevitably presents challenges and frustrations. Beyond the help you get from a mental health professional, it's up to you to look for ways to enhance your overall well-being. There are a number of things you can do to meet life's challenges while fighting depression and to experience greater joy and pleasure in life.

The strategies in this chapter are grounded in the importance of taking good care of your whole being — body, mind and spirit. Adopting these healthy habits can help you recover from depression and reduce your risk of a recurrence. If you haven't experienced depression but are at risk, they may help deter it.

## Getting through the rough times

Treatment for depression generally doesn't produce immediate results. You'll feel better, but it may take time. Here are some suggestions to help you through those initial weeks until your depression begins to ease:

**Don't blame yourself.** Depression is a medical illness — you didn't create it or choose it. The important thing is that you recognize that you need help and that you've started on the road to recovery.

**Follow your treatment plan carefully**. Take your medications as prescribed, and see your doctor regularly. Your doctor can monitor your progress, provide support and encouragement, and adjust your medication if necessary.

**Try not to get discouraged**. It may take a while before you feel back to normal. Keep telling yourself that you will get better.

**Avoid making major life decisions**. Before deciding to embark on a significant transition, such as a career change or a divorce, wait until your depression has cleared and you're confident in your decision-making ability. You don't want life-changing decisions to be influenced by negative thinking associated with depression.

**Simplify your life.** Don't expect to do everything that you usually can do. Put off doing some things if you find them too difficult. Set realistic goals and a reasonable schedule. Find the right balance between doing too little and doing too much. If you do too much too soon, you may feel overwhelmed and become frustrated.

**Get involved.** Take part in activities that make you feel good or like you've achieved something. Even if at first you just show up at an event and don't participate, that's a step in the right direction.

**Acknowledge small steps.** Take satisfaction in even small improvements in your symptoms. Once your treatment starts working, you should have more energy, begin to feel like yourself again and be able to resume some of your normal activities.

As you recover, try some of the measures described in the remainder of this chapter. Even if you can't do everything suggested here, you may be able to incorporate some of these strategies into your daily routine. Do what you're able to and pay attention to what makes you feel good.

## Prescription for healthy living

Regardless of your illness, whether it be depression or another disorder, it's important that you look at the big picture. Getting and staying well involves more than just treating your illness. Good health also includes caring for your entire well-being.

Healthy living strategies are important for everyone. If you've been sick, they're especially important. Eating well and getting plenty of exercise can help you rebuild your strength and energy. Taking care of your emotional and spirituals needs can help reduce stress and other factors that can interfere with a full recovery.

Simply adopting a healthier lifestyle won't cure depression. To treat depression, you need to see a health care professional. But once you begin to feel like your old self again, taking better care of your overall health can help you stay well.

## Caring for your physical health

The cornerstones of good physical health are regular exercise, a nutritious diet and adequate sleep. These healthy habits are important, whether or not you're depressed.

### Keep active

Exercise is an effective way to battle depression. Psychologists at Duke University randomly assigned 156 older adults with mild to moderate major depression to one of three treatments: group exercise three times a week for 45 minutes, antidepressant medication or a combination of both. After 4 months, researchers found that people who exercised showed the same improvement as those who took antidepressants and those who received both treatments. The researchers then followed 83 of the participants for an additional 6 months and found that individuals who continued to exercise regularly were less likely to experience recurrent depression than were those in the other two groups.

Another study found that depressed people who walked, ran or participated in other forms of exercise for 20 to 60 minutes three times a week for as little as 5 weeks experienced noticeable improvements in their mental health. What's more, the benefits lasted up to 1 year.

One way exercise is thought to fight depression is by stimulating the production of endorphins, brain chemicals that produce feelings of satisfaction and wellness. This is the often-referred-to runner's

### Staying motivated

Many people find it difficult to stick with an exercise program. Here are some suggestions to help you stay on track and make exercise part of your daily routine:

**Make it fun.** To prevent boredom, select activities that you enjoy and vary what you do. For example, alternate walking and bicycling with swimming or an aerobics class.

**Set goals.** Start with simple goals and then progress to longer-range goals. People who can stay physically active for 6 months usually end up making regular activity a part of their daily routine. Remember to make your goals realistic and attainable. It's easy to get frustrated and give up if your goals are too ambitious.

**Be flexible.** If you're traveling or have an especially busy day, it's OK to adapt your exercises to accommodate your schedule. If you're sick or injured, take time off from exercise.

**Spend time with others who are physically active.** Physical activity is a great way to build a social support network. Go hiking or canoeing with a friend. Join a softball or golf league. Take a group class such as aerobics or dance. Having exercise partners will help you stay physically active.

**Reward yourself.** After each activity session, take a few minutes to sit down and relax. Savor the good feelings the exercise gives you and think about what you've accomplished. External rewards also can keep you motivated. When you reach one of your goals, treat yourself in some small way.

high. Exercise also provides a host of other benefits:

- It improves your cardiovascular health, reducing your risk of heart disease. This is important because studies suggest depressed people may be at increased risk of heart disease.
- It gives you added energy and improves sleep and appetite.
- It promotes a healthy weight.
- It increases bone mass, reducing your risk of the bone-thinning disease osteoporosis.
- It reduces irritability and anger and produces feelings of mastery and accomplishment.

Both aerobic and nonaerobic forms of exercise are beneficial. Aerobic activities place added demand on your heart, lungs and muscles, increasing your need for oxygen and raising your heart rate and blood pressure. Walking is one of the most convenient forms of aerobic exercise. It's cheap and easy. Other aerobic exercises include bicycling, skiing, tennis, dancing, jogging, swimming and water aerobics. Nonaerobic forms of exercise include strength training (weightlifting) and flexibility exercises, such as stretching and yoga.

Ask your doctor if you should have a physical examination before you begin exercising. When first getting started, begin at an easy pace and gradually increase your time and level of exertion. Aim for 20 to 40 minutes of moderately intense activity most days of the week.

### Eat well

Both your body and your brain need good nutrition to run efficiently. A healthy diet can improve the way you feel on many levels. Eating a variety of foods helps ensure that you get the right mix of nutrients. Experts agree that the best way to increase nutrients in your diet and limit fat and calories is to eat more plant-based foods. Plant foods contain beneficial vitamins, minerals, fiber and health-enhancing compounds called phytochemicals.

For good health and success at maintaining a healthy weight, here are the types and amounts of foods to eat each day. The recommendations are based on the Mayo Clinic Healthy Weight Pyramid, a healthy eating guide.

**Vegetables: Unlimited servings.** Vegetables are naturally low in calories and contain little or no fat. Fresh vegetables are best.

**Fruits: Unlimited servings.** Fruit is generally low in calories and contains little or no fat. Fresh fruit is always best, and it makes a great snack.

**Carbohydrates: 4 to 8 servings.** Carbohydrates include

**Sweets**
Up to 75 calories daily

**Fats**
3 to 5 daily servings

**Protein/Dairy**
3 to 7 daily servings

**Carbohydrates**
4 to 8 daily servings

**Fruits**
Unlimited (minimum 3)

**Vegetables**
Unlimited (minimum 4)

**Mayo Clinic Healthy Weight Pyramid™**

© Mayo Foundation for Medical Education and Research.
See your doctor before you begin any healthy weight plan.

cereals, breads, rice and pasta, and starchy vegetables, such as corn and potatoes. Some foods that are high in carbohydrates are also high in fat and calories, but most plain cereals, breads and pasta are low in fat and calories. Along with vegetables and fruits, carbohydrates should form the foundation of your daily diet.

**Protein/dairy: 3 to 7 servings.** Protein is found in a variety of foods, including milk, yogurt, cheese, eggs, meat, fish and legumes

## Food and mood

For many people, eating is a way of suppressing or soothing negative emotions, such as anger, anxiety or loneliness. To escape emotional eating and drinking:

**Know your triggers.** For several days write down what and when you eat, how you're feeling and how hungry you are. After a while, you may see unhealthy patterns emerge, such as pulling out some ice cream to help soothe an argument with your sister.

**Look elsewhere for comfort.** When you have a craving for sweets or snacks to unwind from a stressful day, take a walk, call a friend or treat yourself to a movie instead.

**Keep high-fat, high-calorie foods out of the house.** Buy just enough of these items to satisfy an occasional small craving. Don't shop when you feel hungry or down.

**Snack smart.** If you feel an urge to eat between meals, limit how much you eat and choose low-fat, low-calorie foods, such as fresh fruit, pretzels or unbuttered popcorn.

**Limit caffeine and sugar.** Some people with depression feel better if they cut out or limit caffeine and sugar in their diet. Caffeine can cause symptoms of anxiety and disrupt sleep. Sugar may provide a temporary energy boost, but afterward it can cause you to feel tired and lethargic.

**Limit alcohol.** It may be tempting to have a few alcoholic drinks, especially if you've had a hard day or are feeling uptight. But this can cause problems because alcohol has a depressant effect. If you drink alcohol, do so in moderation.

If you're taking medications or you have a family history of chemical dependence, it might be best to avoid alcohol altogether. Talk to your doctor about what's best for your situation.

(beans, dried peas and lentils). Try to select fat-free or low-fat varieties of protein.

**Fats: 3 to 5 servings.** Your body needs a small amount of fat to help it function, but most people consume far more fat than they need. An easy way to reduce fat in your diet is to reduce the amount of oil, butter and margarine you add to food when preparing it.

**Sweets: Up to 75 calories daily.** Sweets such as candy and desserts contain considerable calories, may be high in fat and offer little in terms of nutrition. You don't have to give up sweets entirely to eat healthy, but be smart about your selections and portion sizes.

### Get adequate sleep

Sleep refreshes you. It improves your attitude and gives you energy for physical activity and coping with stress. It also boosts your immune system, reducing your risk of illness.

If you're taking medication and having trouble sleeping, talk with your doctor or therapist. Antidepressants can affect sleep in different ways. You may need to change or add a medication. In addition, try these suggestions:

**Establish regular sleep hours.** Go to bed and wake up at the same time each day, including on weekends. Following a regular pattern often improves sleep.

**Relax before bed.** You might practice relaxation techniques (see "Practicing relaxation techniques," page 123), take a warm bath, watch television or listen to soothing music.

**Adopt bedtime rituals.** A regular nightly routine cues your body that it's time for sleep. You might read for a while or have a light snack.

**Limit your time in bed.** Too much sleep promotes shallow, unrestful sleep. Aim for 8 hours of sleep a night. Some people need less, others more. Don't stay in bed longer than 9 hours.

**Don't 'try' to sleep.** The harder you try, the more awake you'll become. Read or watch television until you become drowsy and fall asleep naturally. If you wake up during the night, read or watch TV and turn off the light or TV when you feel sleepy again. Don't get out of bed if possible.

## Finding a healthier addiction

*I have been very heavy my whole life. As a child, I used food to try and obscure my depression. I eat more when I am depressed.*

*When I was 36, I lost 200 pounds and kept it off for a few years. I remember the day I said that nothing was more important than taking this weight off, which for me was a symbol of embracing life. It consciously became my No. 1 priority. I knew I couldn't do it alone. I developed a plan: Weight Watchers, exercise, Overeaters Anonymous and therapy.*

*Exercise, to me, was a well-kept secret. I couldn't believe how good I could feel from working out. Those endorphins are powerful! I'd be at the gym five times a week, for 1 to 2 hours a day. When you're getting rid of one lifetime addiction, sometimes for the first bit you need to replace it with another, healthier addiction.*

*I remember, too, becoming aware of how much I heightened my depression by eating poorly. I'd numb myself with sugar or carbs or fat. Overeaters Anonymous helped me a great deal. Parts of it were very helpful — finding a "higher power" or something to believe in outside myself, and the community of people sharing like feelings.*

Larry

Englewood, New Jersey

**Limit bedroom activities.** Save your bedroom for sleep and sex. Don't bring work to bed.

**Avoid or limit caffeine, alcohol and nicotine.** Caffeine and nicotine can keep you from falling asleep. Alcohol causes unrestful sleep and frequent awakenings.

**Minimize interruptions.** Close your bedroom door or create a subtle background noise, such as a fan, to drown out other noises. Keep your bedroom temperature comfortable — cool temperatures help induce sleep. Drink less fluid before bed so that you won't have to get up at night to go to the bathroom.

**Keep active.** Regular physical activity helps you sleep more soundly. Try to exercise 4 to 5 hours before you go to bed. Exercising too close to bedtime can keep you awake.

## Boosting your emotional health

Depression isn't just about brain chemicals and hormone levels. It affects your emotions, thoughts, beliefs and attitudes. Even after you've recovered from an episode of depression, you're still going to experience difficult and painful emotions from time to time, including feelings of anger and sadness. Learning healthy ways of dealing with powerful feelings and beliefs can help you manage your emotional well-being.

### Managing your anger

It's natural to feel angry once in a while. Someone cuts you off in traffic. You get stuck with a dreaded task at work. A co-worker is rude to you. But it's not healthy to stay angry, bottle up your anger or express it with explosive outbursts. Mismanaged anger can hurt you in many ways. The following steps can help you deal with anger more positively:

**Identify your anger triggers.** If a visiting friend usually manages to rile you, knowing this ahead of time can help you prepare for the next visit. If you get angry when you run late for appointments, plan more time for travel.

**Recognize signs of emerging anger.** What do you do when you start to get angry? Do your neck and shoulders tighten up? Do you clench your teeth? Do you speak more quickly or louder? Read these symptoms as a warning that you need to calm down.

**Take time to cool down.** When you find yourself becoming angry, take a short timeout. Walk away from the situation until you calm down. Count to 10, take a few deep breaths, look out a window, slowly repeat a calming word or phrase.

**Choose how to respond to the situation.** You have a choice about how to respond to situations. With practice, you can choose to express your anger in appropriate and nonaggressive ways.

**Find release valves.** Look for creative ways to release the energy produced by your anger, such as writing, listening to music, dancing or painting.

**Don't unleash your anger.** Express your frustration calmly rather than verbally attacking the person. For example, you might say, "I feel hurt by what you said," rather than, "You insulted me for the 20th time today!"

**Release 'hot thoughts.'** Notice and release irrational thoughts that kindle anger. Instead of telling yourself, "This is terrible, everything's ruined," say, "It's frustrating, and it's understandable that I'm upset, but it's not the end of the world."

## Practicing forgiveness

Anger may be fueled by a lingering resentment toward someone who wronged you or hurt you. Researchers believe that harboring vengeful and painful feelings toward someone places your body under ongoing stress. Holding on to anger may increase your risk of high blood pressure and heart disease, in addition to harming your emotional health.

How do you let go of anger? You try to forgive. A study of women who survived incest found that those who learned to forgive lessened their anxiety and depression. Forgiving someone who has hurt you could be one of the hardest things you ever do. Forgiving doesn't mean forgetting, denying, condoning or reconciling. Rather, it's a way to keep negative feelings from consuming you.

Forgiveness involves four phases. First, you acknowledge your pain. Next, you recognize that something has to change if you're to heal. This is followed by the work phase, the really hard part. You strive to find a new way to think about the person who hurt you. Last, you begin to experience emotional relief. As your pain lessens, you're able to move forward.

## Coping with grief

Losing something or someone important to you is a wrenching experience. You can't avoid losses — everyone faces them — but you can approach grief in ways that reduce your risk of developing depression from the loss. To overcome grief:

**Let yourself feel the loss.** Recognize it as serious. Don't try to hide from your feelings. When you're choked up, have a good cry. Even strong men and women cry.

**Express your feelings to others.** Talk to supportive family and friends, your doctor or a counselor.

**Ask for help.** Your friends may want to help but don't know what to do. Tell them what you need, whether it's a meal, a ride or a shoulder to cry on.

**Give yourself time for healing.** Grief is a process. You may feel numb, empty and lost for weeks or months, but eventually you'll feel a stronger sense of direction. If your grief is severe or persists for a year, discuss your feelings and symptoms with your doctor.

### Keeping an optimistic outlook

All of us silently talk to ourselves, commenting on how we look and act and mulling over problems. Self-talk is the endless stream of thoughts that run through your head every day. These automatic thoughts may be positive or negative. People who are depressed are more likely to have negative thoughts.

With practice you can learn to identify negative thoughts and replace them with positive ones. Throughout the day, stop and evaluate what you're thinking and find a way to put a positive spin on your negative thoughts. Over time, your self-talk will automatically become more positive and rational. These tips also may help:

- Realize that bad situations often are temporary. Like rainy weather, many bad situations clear up in time.
- Don't always blame yourself when something goes wrong. If your spouse, friend or boss is in a bad mood, don't assume it's because of something you did.
- Think about how you can improve a bad situation. If a co-worker is critical of your work, ask for positive feedback on how to make improvements.
- Before you give in to negative thoughts, ask yourself: "Am I overreacting?"

### Starting a journal

Writing in a journal can help you express pain, anger and fears, increase your self-awareness and help you put things in perspective. Studies also suggest health benefits from journaling. Experts believe writing about feelings and events helps relieve stress.

Keep your journal private. It's easier to write honestly if only you will read it. Rather than recording daily events, focus on your feelings. This will help ease anxiety, help you work through painful feelings and give you the most benefit. If you experience an intense emotion, positive or negative, write down the circumstances and the effects of the experience. Because facing and expressing your emotions may briefly increase distress, it's best not to write in your journal at bedtime.

### Controlling stress

Some people are more stress resistant than others. Although they confront the same stresses as anyone else, they seem to handle the strain with less difficulty. If you get stressed easily, do you know why? Sometimes simply becoming aware of what causes you stress can make the stress easier to deal with. Your stress may be linked to external factors such as work, family or unpredictable events. Or it may stem from internal factors, such as perfectionism or un-realistic expectations.

Ask yourself if you can do anything to lessen or avoid your sources of stress. Some stressors you can control, others you can't. Concentrate on those stressors that you can change. For situations that are beyond your control, look for ways to remain calm under the circumstances. Here are suggestions for limiting daily stress:

**Plan your day.** You might start by getting up 15 minutes earlier to ease the morning rush. Keep a written schedule of your daily activities so that you don't run into conflicts or last minute rushes to get to an appointment or activity.

**Simplify your schedule.** Prioritize, plan and pace yourself. Learn to delegate responsibility to others. Say no to added respon-sibilities or commitments if you're not up to doing them.

**Get organized.** Organize your home and work space so that you know where things are and can easily reach them.

**Change the pace.** Break away from your routine once in a while and explore new territory without a schedule. Take a vacation, even if it's just a weekend getaway.

**Recognize stress signals.** Is your back bothering you? Do you find yourself misplacing things or speeding when driving? When you see early warnings of stress, force yourself to stop and say, "I'm under stress, and I need to do something about it."

### Practicing relaxation techniques

Relaxation helps produce a physical and mental state of calm that's the opposite of the fight-or-flight response triggered by stress. Relaxation not only helps relieve stress but also helps you handle daily demands and remain alert, energetic and productive. Many techniques promote relaxation. Here are some to get you started:

**Deep breathing.** Most adults breathe shallowly from their chest. Deep breathing from your diaphragm, the muscle between your chest and abdomen, is relaxing. Sit comfortably with your feet flat on the floor. Loosen tight clothing around your abdomen and waist. Place your hands in your lap or at your sides. Breathe in slowly — through your nose, if possible — while counting to four. Allow your abdomen to expand as you breathe in. Pause for a second and then exhale at a normal rate through your mouth.

**Progressive muscle relaxation.** This technique involves relaxing a series of muscles one at a time by increasing and then decreasing the tension in the muscles. First, gently tighten or clench a group of muscles, such as those in a leg or an arm, and then relax them. Concentrate on letting the tension go in each muscle. Then move on to the next group. You can start with toes and feet, for example, and move up through the legs, buttocks, back, abdomen, chest, shoulders, arms, hands, and so on.

**Meditation.** People have been meditating for centuries in many religious and cultural traditions. There's no single right way to meditate. Most forms involve sitting quietly for 15 to 20 minutes while breathing slowly and rhythmically. It's helpful to have someone guide you through your first meditation sessions. Meditation or yoga instructors and some therapists can teach you. Meditation tapes and compact discs also are available.

**Guided imagery.** Guided imagery, also known as visualization, is a method of relaxation that involves sitting or lying quietly and picturing yourself in a peaceful setting. You experience the setting with all of your senses as if you were actually there. For instance, imagine lying on the beach. Picture the beautiful blue sky, feel the warmth of the sun and the breeze on your skin, smell the salt water and hear the pounding of the surf. The messages your brain receives as you imagine these sensations help you to relax.

## Getting involved

Years of research show that a strong social network is an important component of overall health. People who feel connected to others tend to be healthier physically. They have a stronger immune system and less risk of illness and death.

Social ties also improve your mental health, giving you a sense of purpose or meaning. Good friends and a supportive family can provide encouraging words, offer gentle but helpful feedback and lend a hand when you need help. They can also motivate you to take better care of yourself. Examine your social support network.

### What about support groups?

Some people find comfort in talking with people who share similar feelings and concerns. Besides offering emotional support, these groups can give you a sense of belonging or fitting in. They can also provide an opportunity to meet new friends.

However, support groups aren't for everyone. To benefit from a support group, you have to be willing to share your thoughts and feelings honestly. You must also be willing to learn about and help others. People who are uncomfortable talking in front of a group or listening to other people's problems are less likely to benefit. Keep in mind, though, that it's normal to feel a bit nervous about joining a new group of people or talking in front of them. Don't let this stop you. Many people discover after a couple of sessions that they enjoy the meetings and find them helpful.

To find out if there's a support group in your area for people experiencing depression, check with your doctor or therapist. You might also check with your county health department, a community health organization or your local library. You can also contact the mental health organizations listed on page 185. Avoid groups that promise quick fixes or force you to talk about things you're not comfortable discussing.

Many support groups exist on the Internet. An online group might be helpful if you live in a rural area or a small community. But keep in mind that interaction via the computer is no substitute for face-to-face communication. Plus, you can't always be certain that the people you're chatting with are who they claim to be.

If it needs bolstering, consider some of these ideas:

**Make time for your extended family.** Plan a reunion with your grandparents, parents, sisters and brothers. Re-establish ties with a favorite aunt or a long-lost cousin.

**Meet your neighbors.** Schedule a neighborhood picnic or a block party. When you see your neighbors outside, introduce yourself.

**Join community organizations.** Build ties with other people who care about similar issues.

**Respond to others.** Accept invitations to events. Answer phone calls and letters. Be a good listener.

**Set aside differences.** Approach your relationships with a clean slate, even if you've had difficulties in the past.

## Attending to your spiritual needs

Spirituality is often confused with religion. But spirituality isn't so much connected to a specific belief or form of worship as it is with the spirit or the soul. Spirituality is about meaning, values and purpose in life. Religion is one way of expressing spiritual beliefs, but it's not the only way. For some people, spirituality is feeling in tune with nature. Others express their spirituality through music or art.

### Spirituality and healing

Numerous studies have attempted to measure the effect of spirituality on illness and recovery. Most of these studies suggest that spiritual beliefs have a beneficial effect on health. No one knows exactly how spirituality affects health. It may be from the healing effect of hope, known to help your immune system. A practice such as meditation, which is part of many spiritual traditions, can decrease muscle tension and lower your heart rate. Other researchers point to social connections that spirituality often provides.

Although spirituality is associated with healing and better health, it isn't a cure. Spirituality can help you live life more fully despite your symptoms, but studies haven't found that it actually cures health problems. It's best to view spirituality as a helpful healing force, but not a substitute for traditional medical care.

### Finding spiritual well-being

To rejuvenate the spiritual side of your life, identify what brings you inner peace. You may find it through one of the following:

- Inspirational writings
- Worship
- Prayer or meditation
- Art
- Music
- Spending time outdoors

## The best defense is a good offense

One of the best ways to manage depression and prevent recurrent episodes is to anticipate and solve potential problems before they become problems. This means sticking to your treatment plan and embracing habits that support your recovery, such as exercise. It also means staying alert to warning signs of a recurrence.

Warning signs will be different for everyone. Maybe you've started waking up early in the morning, or you're eating more than usual. You might feel particularly irritable, flying off the handle over trivial matters. Stay attuned to your own red flags, signs that you may be getting depressed.

Remember that life naturally brings ups and downs — occasionally feeling sad or blue doesn't mean you're sinking into another depression. But if these feelings persist, see your doctor or therapist. He or she may suggest a change in your treatment plan or remind you how to use coping skills you've already learned.

# Part 3

*Special Groups and Concerns*

## Chapter 11

# Women and depression

D epression is twice as common in women as it is in men. Over the course of a lifetime, approximately 20 percent of women will experience major depression or dysthymia, compared with 10 percent of men. With bipolar disorder, prevalence of the illness is about equal between men and women, although women typically have more depressive episodes and fewer manic episodes.

Depression generally affects women at an earlier age — most often between 25 and 44 — than it affects men. Signs and symptoms of depression also tend to be different in women than in men. Women more often experience an increased appetite, weight gain and carbohydrate cravings. Men tend to lose both appetite and weight when depressed. Women are also more likely to develop seasonal depression or to experience an accompanying condition, such as an anxiety or eating disorder. Depressed men are at greater risk of substance abuse.

## Why are women more vulnerable?

A variety of medical, psychological and social factors unique to women's lives are thought to account for depression's being more common in women than in men. The following factors likely interact to increase women's risk of becoming depressed:

**Biological factors.** These may include genetic factors and mood changes associated with the production of female sex hormones.

**Social and cultural factors.** Women are more likely to shoulder the burden of both work and family responsibilities. They're also more likely than are men to experience poverty and single parenthood and to have a history of sexual or physical abuse.

**Psychological factors.** Women and men may learn to handle emotions and cope with stress in different ways. Some experts propose that because of social and cultural factors, women are less inclined than men to act on their problems, but more inclined to dwell on them.

## Depression during the reproductive years

Before girls and boys enter adolescence, they have similar rates of depression. With puberty, differences begin to develop. Between the ages of 11 and 13, depression rates for girls jump dramatically. By age 15, females are almost twice as likely as males to experience a major depressive episode.

Because this gender gap develops after puberty and disappears following menopause, scientists believe hormonal factors are involved. Women's physical experiences during their reproductive years — including menstruation, pregnancy and menopause — bring fluctuations in the production of sex hormones that can be associated with mood changes. Hormonal changes — especially when combined with other medical factors or with psychological or social issues — may increase a woman's risk of depression.

## Premenstrual dysphoric disorder

Millions of women know all too well the changes in mood that can occur just before menstruation: anxiety, irritability and sadness. Twenty percent to 40 percent of women experience these emotions.

Many women also experience physical symptoms just before menstruation, such as bloating, breast pain, fatigue, muscle aches or headache.

For a small percentage of women — 3 percent to 5 percent — premenstrual symptoms are so severe that they disrupt their life and relationships. This condition is called premenstrual dysphoric disorder (PMDD). Symptoms of PMDD can include:

- Markedly depressed mood
- Feelings of hopelessness
- Anxiety, tension, feelings of being keyed up or on edge
- Tearfulness
- Increased sensitivity to personal rejection
- Uncharacteristic anger or irritability and increased conflicts with others
- Decreased interest in usual activities
- Difficulty concentrating
- Lethargy, fatigue, lack of energy
- Change in appetite and sleep patterns
- Feelings of being overwhelmed or out of control

Researchers are studying what makes some women susceptible to PMDD. Physical and emotional changes that commonly occur before menopause are thought to result from a heightened response to normal hormonal changes. PMDD, on the other hand, may stem from an abnormal response to hormonal changes.

Selective serotonin reuptake inhibitors (SSRIs) often are effective in treating symptoms of PMDD. Usually these medications are taken daily. They may also be taken only during the 2 weeks before menstruation begins, when PMDD typically develops. Your doctor can help determine which method is best for you. Other treatments for PMDD include increased exercise, dietary changes, relaxation techniques and psychotherapy.

## Depression during pregnancy

Many women feel especially healthy and positive during pregnancy. Increased production of certain hormones seems to give them a mental boost. However, about 10 percent of women experience depression during pregnancy. The risk is greatest for women who have a history of depression. Other risk factors include a history of PMDD, limited social support, a young age, living alone, marital conflicts and ambivalence about being pregnant.

Deciding how to treat depression during pregnancy involves weighing the risks and benefits of various therapies with your doctor. The self-care strategies described in Chapter 10 may be helpful for mild depression. For moderate depression, psychotherapy may be beneficial.

If you have moderate to severe depression that's interfering with your ability to care for yourself, you may benefit from taking an antidepressant. Research suggests that SSRIs are relatively safe for both the mother and the fetus during pregnancy. The majority of recent studies of women who took SSRIs during pregnancy found the medications didn't harm the fetus. Your doctor can help you weigh the pros and cons for your situation.

Many women prefer — and their doctors advise them — to avoid medications during pregnancy. But the risks of not treating depression, especially its more severe forms, must be considered. They can include poor nutrition for the mother and fetus, inadequate prenatal care, low infant birth weight and premature birth. Untreated depression can also lead to chronic or more severe depression. Depressed women who discontinue antidepressant medication early in their pregnancy show a 50 percent relapse rate by the third trimester, according to an ongoing study at the University of California at Los Angeles and Emory University.

For women with severe depression that doesn't improve with other treatments, electroconvulsive therapy (ECT) may be an option. Although used infrequently during pregnancy, ECT is considered relatively safe.

## Postpartum depression

Having a baby is a powerful, exciting, frightening and joyous event. It's common for women to experience a wide range of emotions following the birth of their child, including symptoms known as the baby blues. Within a few days of giving birth, more than half of new mothers feel sad, angry, irritable or anxious. New mothers may cry for no apparent reason and may even have negative thoughts about their baby. These feelings are normal and generally subside within a week or so.

A more severe condition following childbirth, called postpartum depression, affects up to 25 percent of new mothers. This type of depression likely stems from a deficiency of, or change in, sex hormones that affects brain activity in regions involved in regulating mood. Symptoms of postpartum depression are similar to those of major depression and usually develop within weeks after giving birth. In addition, you may feel a lack of concern for yourself or your baby or an excessive concern for the baby. You may have unreasonably high expectations of yourself or feel trapped. You might feel inadequate and question your ability to be a parent.

You're at increased risk of experiencing postpartum depression if you:
- Have a history of depression
- Experience depression during pregnancy
- Experience marital problems
- Undergo difficult life events during pregnancy
- Lack a social support system

Treatment for postpartum depression may include antidepressant medications, psychotherapy or both. A concern among mothers who breast-feed is that taking antidepressants puts their baby at risk. Studies haven't found adverse effects from SSRIs in breast-fed infants, but more research is still needed to assess possible long-term effects. Some researchers believe estrogen supplements also may be effective in treating postpartum depression. Additional research is needed in this area as well.

## Menopause and depression

Signs and symptoms of menopause generally begin before the end of menstruation and may persist for up to a year afterward. This

## A firsthand account of postpartum depression

*As a new mother at age 38, I had never heard of postpartum depression. For the first few weeks, I was without the melancholy that follows birth, the baby blues. But anxiety was at an all-time high, and nothing could have prepared me for the initially frightening prospect of taking care of another life.*

*I remember the long nights I lay in wait of elusive sleep. This was nothing like the occasional insomnia I'd suffered during job-related stress, excitement about a trip or even the last month of pregnancy. Ironically, our infant son slept nearly through the night from the start.*

*After a few weeks of taking over-the-counter sleep aids, I began a roller coaster of visits to doctors. Recognizing my fears surrounding motherhood, I also saw a psychologist, who became a major source of support for the next few months and a constant in a whirlwind of emotions, doctors and medications.*

*Three months after my son's birth, I felt pretty good and decided to taper off the antidepressant that had probably just begun working. I wanted to prove I was strong and didn't need pills. The insomnia reappeared a few weeks after I'd stopped the medication and a few days before my mother was diagnosed with cancer. I was pretty naive about depression and its treatment and was overwhelmed by the prospect of losing my mother. My mother died on Christmas morning when our son was almost 5 months old. The next few months were very bleak.*

*Eventually one of my doctors said, "You don't have to be ashamed to take an antidepressant. I do." From his sharing this simple confidence, I respected this doctor for exposing his humanness.*

*Fortunately, I have a very supportive, loving and kind husband. Also critical to my recovery was staying on the medication, exercising and spending many days with the baby at my neighbors' homes. In-laws and friends became closer, sharing in their own life trials, which in turn gave me hope to get better.*

Brenda

Hudson, Wisconsin

transitional period, when hormone levels often fluctuate, is called perimenopause. During this time many women experience a variety of changes in body function and emotions, including hot flashes, sleep difficulties and mood swings.

Menopause or perimenopause alone don't cause depression. However, women who are at increased risk of depression because of other genetic or life factors may experience depression during their menopausal and perimenopausal years, when their hormone levels are fluctuating.

### Hormone replacement therapy

Studies show that hormone replacement therapy (HRT), which is commonly prescribed to relieve symptoms associated with menopause, may improve mood in women with mild depression. Supplemental estrogen in HRT can also help relieve hot flashes and sleep difficulties, and it can help prevent the bone-thinning disease osteoporosis. A study sponsored by the National Institute of Mental Health examined the association between depression and hormone levels. It found that mineral density in the hipbones of women with a history of major depression was 10 percent to 15 percent lower than normal for their age. Reduced bone density increases a woman's risk of hip fracture.

Hormone replacement therapy alone generally isn't enough to treat moderate to severe depression. Your doctor may recommend combining hormone therapy with an antidepressant medication, psychotherapy or both. It's generally safe to take both HRT and an antidepressant medication.

## Social and cultural issues

It's not just biology that accounts for women's higher rates of depression. Women may face social and cultural stresses that increase their risk of depression. These stresses also occur in men, but generally at a lower rate.

**Unequal power and status.** In general, women earn less money and hold less power than do men. Three-fourths of the people living in poverty in the United States today are women and children. Low socioeconomic status brings with it many concerns and stresses, including uncertainty about the future and less access to community and medical resources. Minority women may also face stress from racial discrimination.

When individuals — women or men — feel they don't have control of their life, they may experience certain emotions, such as passivity, negativism and lack of self-esteem, that put them at increased risk of depression.

**Work overload.** When considering that many women hold jobs away from home and that women generally handle the majority of domestic chores at home, women often work more hours a week than do men. In addition, many women find themselves dealing with the challenges and stresses that can accompany single parenthood. Women may also find themselves sandwiched between generations — caring for their young children and caring for sick and older family members.

**Sexual and physical abuse.** Studies show that women molested as children are more likely to experience depression at some point in their life than women who weren't molested as children. Studies also show a higher incidence of depression among women who were raped as teenagers or young adults. Although sexual abuse also occurs in boys and young men, it's more common among girls and young women

Adult women may also experience domestic abuse — severe or ongoing physical violence, mental abuse or both — from a partner, a spouse or another family member. According to the latest Department of Justice figures, of the 1 million cases of intimate partner violence that occurred in 1998, 85 percent involved violence against women.

Sexual and physical abuse can result in loss of self-esteem and self-worth and it can lead to conditions such as post-traumatic stress disorder.

## Taking control

The daily stresses of life can leave some women feeling as if they're caught in a desperate cycle. The following suggestions can help you to better cope with stress and feel more in control:

**Get active.** Regular exercise promotes self-confidence and provides feelings of mastery. It also improves sleep and gives you energy to deal with daily events.

**Branch out.** Get involved in different activities and settings. If things aren't going well in one area, such as your home life, you can still feel satisfied with your successes in other areas, such as work or community projects. When you feel down, shift your attention to an area that gives you a stronger sense of control over your life.

**Make time for yourself.** In addition to caring for others, you need to care for yourself. Each day, reserve some time for yourself to relax or take part in activities that you enjoy.

**Think positive.** Try to accept the stresses of life as the way things are. Find ways to live with or change them rather than worrying about them.

**Seek support.** Develop a network of friends or family members that can support one another through stressful times. If you're involved in an abusive relationship, contact health or social service professionals for guidance and support in how to improve or get out of the relationship.

## With help comes hope

Women may be more vulnerable to depression, but they generally respond well to treatment. Even severe depression often can be successfully treated.

Believing that your condition is hopeless or incurable may be associated with your depression or with situations in life in which you had little control or influence. Don't let these feelings keep you from getting professional help. Treating depression can be a first step in changing and improving your life. As you begin to feel better about yourself, you'll gain self-confidence and find the energy and willpower to master your challenges. Many women who successfully overcome depression go on to enjoy pleasurable and productive lives.

## Chapter 12

# *Older adults and depression*

Some people mistakenly believe that depression is a natural part of aging. Depression isn't inevitable as you get older. But many factors in life that come with older age, including increased health problems, financial stress, and the death of family members and friends, can increase risk of depression. Approximately 15 percent of older Americans — about 6 million men and women age 65 and older — experience depression.

Once it's recognized, depression can often be effectively treated. Older adults generally respond as well to treatment as do younger individuals.

## Common triggers

Among older adults, the following medical, psychological and social factors may contribute to the development of depression:

**Physical illness.** Depression can occur with conditions more common later in life, such as Alzheimer's disease, Parkinson's disease, stroke, heart disease and cancer. Because symptoms of these diseases may overlap with those of depression, depression is often underdiagnosed in older adults with other health problems.

**Medications.** Some medications can trigger depression. Others can make you more vulnerable to depression by altering your hormone levels or interacting with other medications. Still other medications can cause fatigue. Fatigue may lead to lack of exercise, poor nutrition and social isolation — factors that can trigger depression. Some people also misuse their medications — intentionally or unintentionally — or combine them with alcohol, which is a depressant. This can also increase your risk of depression.

**Grief.** With increasing age you're more likely to experience the death of a spouse, family member or friend and the sadness and grief that accompanies death.

**Retirement.** In 1900 two-thirds of men over age 65 were still employed. In 1990 only 16 percent of men and 7 percent of women were still working outside the home beyond age 65. As people retire earlier and life expectancy increases, there's a longer period between the end of a career and the end of life. Many older adults make a smooth transition from working to retirement. But some have more difficulty, especially those who derive their self-esteem and satisfaction from their careers. Retirement may also mean a move to a new location and the loss of well-established ties.

**Reflection.** With age you tend to reflect on your life and your accomplishments. Some people become saddened from a sense of not having fulfilled their life expectations, or they become disappointed that they didn't do things differently in their life.

**Confronting mortality.** Some people have difficulty accepting that their life may be nearing an end.

## Recognizing depression in older adults

Unrecognized and untreated depression can have serious consequences on quality of life. It can lead to decreased physical functioning and an increased reliance on others. Depression may even be associated with an increased risk of early death among people with certain forms of heart disease, including heart rhythm disturbances (arrhythmia) and reduced blood flow to the heart (coronary artery disease).

With age it can become more difficult to recognize depression. You or your doctor may attribute symptoms of depression, such as low energy, memory and concentration changes, uncharacteristic irritability, loss of appetite and troubles sleeping, to the effects of an illness. Additionally, like many older adults, you may have grown up in an era when a stigma was associated with any type of mental illness. If so, you may talk of aches or pains but not mention feeling sad, helpless or worthless. Other changes associated with late-life depression include loss of interest in usual activities, increased alcohol use, social withdrawal, increased anxiety and being suspicious of others.

## Alzheimer's, Parkinson's and depression

Two fairly common diseases in older adults are Alzheimer's disease and Parkinson's disease. Because certain symptoms associated with these diseases may be similar to those of depression, sometimes it can be difficult to determine if a person has early Alzheimer's disease, early Parkinson's disease, depression or a combination of these illnesses. For these reasons, a psychiatrist is often part of the team making the diagnosis.

### Alzheimer's disease and depression

Identifying if an individual is depressed, has early Alzheimer's disease or both is important in determining the best treatment. The following list of some of the differences between depression and early Alzheimer's disease can help in the diagnosis:

- An individual with depression may make little effort to perform well on tests doctors use to assess memory. A person who isn't depressed but may have Alzheimer's disease usually cooperates and tries to perform the tasks to the best of his or her ability.
- An individual who's depressed may not enjoy normally pleasurable or interesting experiences. An individual with early Alzheimer's disease usually continues to enjoy activities that he or she finds pleasurable or interesting.
- An individual experiencing depression continues to speak and understand language and is able to perform well-learned

motor activities without difficulty. A person with early Alzheimer's disease may begin to have difficulty speaking, naming objects, writing or understanding language. He or she may also have some difficulty performing common motor activities, such as getting dressed.

- A depressed person often responds well to antidepressant therapy. A person with early Alzheimer's disease that's not accompanied by depression generally doesn't respond to antidepressants. A person with both early Alzheimer's disease and depression may show some improvement with antidepressant medication. Symptoms of depression may improve, but the medication doesn't treat features of Alzheimer's disease.

### Parkinson's disease and depression

Approximately 40 percent of people with Parkinson's disease also develop depression. In about one in four of these individuals, symptoms of depression may occur months or even years before Parkinson's disease is diagnosed. Although physical limitations resulting from Parkinson's disease can be frustrating and stressful, depression in someone with Parkinson's disease generally isn't a reaction to physical disability. It more likely arises from underlying brain changes associated with Parkinson's disease.

Like Alzheimer's disease, diagnosing depression in someone with Parkinson's disease can be difficult because symptoms of the two illnesses — loss of energy, inability to sleep, slow movements and quiet speech — may be similar. One way to tell the difference between symptoms of Parkinson's disease and depression is appetite. People with Parkinson's disease who aren't depressed generally have good appetites, even though they may lose weight.

Another distinction is interest in, and enjoyment from, certain activities. Although someone with Parkinson's disease may get frustrated by his or her physical limitations and, as a result, avoid doing certain things, he or she is still interested in the activities. A depressed person, on the other hand, generally no longer partakes in once enjoyable activities because he or she no longer finds them interesting or pleasurable.

## Stroke and depression

Stroke results when a blood vessel in the brain ruptures or becomes blocked, injuring brain tissue. It commonly occurs in older adults and can cause mild to severe complications. Depending on which part of the brain is involved, different patterns of muscle weakness, speech difficulty and memory impairment may result.

There's also a strong link between stroke and depression. Up to half the people who experience a stroke develop depression within 2 years of the stroke. Risk of depression doesn't coincide with the degree of physical difficulties from the stroke. Some individuals with mild physical difficulties may become depressed, whereas others with severe physical difficulties don't experience depression. Research suggests that one predictor of subsequent depression is the location of the stroke. Strokes in the left, front portion of the brain may be more likely to lead to depression than strokes in other brain regions.

Like other forms of depression, depression that follows a stroke can often be effectively treated with medication, psychotherapy or both. Unfortunately, depression is often missed in this group of people. Doctors, family members and people recovering from a stroke may mistakenly assume depressive symptoms are "normal" in these circumstances. One reason treating depression is important is because effective treatment can enhance an individual's ability to recover from the physical effects of the stroke.

## Treating depression in older adults

More than 80 percent of depressed older adults improve with treatment. Antidepressants are commonly used. They're generally effective, and most people experience few, if any, side effects, especially with newer antidepressants. To reduce your risk of side effects, your doctor may recommend starting with a lower dose of the medication and slowly increasing the dose. Lower doses of antidepressants may be adequate because with age your body tends to metabolize medications more slowly.

Psychotherapy also is often beneficial and may be the first line of treatment for mild to moderate depression, especially if a doctor is concerned about possible side effects or drug interactions from adding another medication to the mix of medications you're already taking. Electroconvulsive therapy (ECT) is generally recommended if you have moderate to severe depression and haven't responded to other treatments. ECT is safe and often as effective in older adults as in younger adults.

## Managing depression

Once your symptoms are under control and you're feeling better, the following steps may help prevent another depressive episode. (They may also help prevent a first episode of depression.) Other strategies for managing depression are listed in Chapter 10.

**Renew and form new relationships.** With retirement you and your spouse may be together a lot more than you're used to. That means you might have to readjust your routines and expectations. Your relationships with your family members and friends also may change. View these changes as opportunities.

**Keep socially active.** Go out to coffee with friends. Plan activities with neighbors and relatives. If you're feeling restless, learn a new hobby, take a computer course or volunteer at a local organization. If you live alone and don't have many social contacts, investigate available community resources or consider moving to a retirement community that provides a better opportunity for socializing.

**Keep physically active.** If your health allows, take a daily walk. You might also join a fitness class for seniors or sign up for a golf league. But check with your doctor first to make sure it's safe for you to increase your level of physical activity.

**Use your medications wisely.** Take all of your medications as prescribed by your doctor. And make sure to inform your doctor and pharmacist of all of the medications you take.

## Chapter 13

# *Childhood and teenage depression*

In the last 20 years, health care professionals have made a concerted effort to recognize and better understand mood disorders in children and teenagers. At one time doctors believed that children and teenagers didn't have the mental maturity to experience depression. But researchers are finding that depression is common in children and teens, that young people are prone to the same types of depression as adults, and in this age group depression often isn't recognized and treated.

Consider these basic facts:

- Depression may occur in as many as 1 in 33 children and 1 in 8 teenagers in the United States. At any given time, as many as 3 percent of children and teens are depressed.
- Once a child or a teenager has an episode of depression, he or she has a greater than 50 percent chance of experiencing another episode in the next 5 years.
- Two-thirds of youth with mental illnesses don't get the help they need.
- Suicide is the third leading cause of death for 15- to 24-year-olds and the sixth leading cause of death for 5- to 15-year-olds.
- The rate of suicide for 5- to 24-year-olds has tripled since 1960.

When children and teenagers live with untreated depression, family relationships can suffer, social development may be affected, they may do poorly in school, they may abuse alcohol or drugs, and they may be at risk of suicide. The good news is, prompt identification and treatment of childhood and teenage depression can reduce its duration and severity, and the risk of complications.

## What to watch for

By and large, depression in children and teenagers is diagnosed using the same criteria as in adults. But how depressive symptoms present themselves can differ between young people and adults. It can be challenging to recognize depression in children and teens because the symptoms may be difficult to detect or easy to attribute to something else, like a growing phase or hormonal changes.

In addition, many behaviors associated with depression in young people can be normal reactions in children and teenagers. For example, almost all youth argue with their parents or teachers or refuse to do chores from time to time. It's the number of symptoms that a child or a teenager displays, the duration of the symptoms and their severity that a mental health professional takes into account in determining if a child or a teenager is depressed. The lists below show how a young person in each of three different age groups may exhibit depression:

**A preschooler:**
- Is listless
- Isn't interested in playing
- Cries easily and more frequently

**A child in elementary school:**
- Is listless and moody
- Is more irritable than usual
- Has a sad appearance
- Is easily discouraged
- Complains of being bored
- Is more distant with family and friends
- Has difficulty with schoolwork
- Talks about death a lot

**A teenager:**
- Is always tired
- Drops out of favorite activities
- Has more arguments with his or her parents and teachers
- Refuses to do chores or homework
- Engages in harmful behavior, such as cutting himself or herself
- Has suicidal thoughts

Like adults, children and teenagers also can develop a type of depression that's different (atypical) from other depression in that their mood may improve for short periods, and they're able to experience some joy in response to positive events. This contrasts more common forms of depression in which mood tends to be consistently sad and not easily influenced by positive events.

## Is your child at risk?

As children, both boys and girls seem to run the same risk of depression. When they reach their teenage years, however, girls become twice as likely as boys to experience depression. Females remain at a higher risk of depression through middle age.

Research suggests that genes, female sex hormones, psychological issues and social stresses all may be linked to the increased rate of depression among teenage girls. Genetics may be especially important, as youth who experience depression often have a parent who developed depression at an early age. Depressed teenagers are also more likely to have a family history of the illness.

In addition to family history, these factors may increase the risk of depression in a child or a teenager:
- Experiencing significant stress
- Being the victim of abuse or neglect
- Experiencing the death of a parent or other loved one
- Breaking up with someone
- Having a chronic illness, such as diabetes
- Experiencing other trauma
- Having a behavior or learning disorder

### A depression checklist for parents

Below are signs and symptoms of depression common in children and teenagers. You can use the lists to help you gather information about your child's feelings, thinking, physical problems, behavior problems and suicide risk.

**Feelings — Does your child demonstrate the following:**
- ☐ Sadness
- ☐ Emptiness
- ☐ Hopelessness
- ☐ Guilt
- ☐ Worthlessness
- ☐ Lack of enjoyment in everyday pleasures

**Thinking — Is your child having trouble:**
- ☐ Concentrating
- ☐ Making decisions
- ☐ Completing schoolwork
- ☐ Maintaining grades
- ☐ Maintaining friendships

**Physical problems — Does your child complain of:**
- ☐ Headaches
- ☐ Stomachaches
- ☐ Lack of energy

## Related conditions

Children and teenagers who experience depression often have another mental illness. Mental illnesses that can occur with depression include:

**An eating disorder.** Girls are more likely to develop the eating disorders anorexia nervosa or bulimia nervosa than are boys. Many teenagers with anorexia nervosa are significantly depressed. They see themselves as fat, even if they're dangerously thin. Controlling

❏ Sleeping problems (too much or too little)
❏ Weight or appetite changes (gain or loss)

**Behavior problems — Is your child:**
❏ Irritable
❏ Not wanting to go to school
❏ Wanting to be alone most of the time
❏ Having difficulty getting along with others
❏ Cutting classes or skipping school
❏ Dropping out of sports, hobbies or other activities
❏ Drinking alcohol or using drugs

**Suicide risk — Does your child talk or think about:**
❏ Suicide
❏ Death
❏ Other morbid subjects

If your child experiences five or more of these signs or symptoms for at least 2 weeks, he or she may be experiencing depression or another mental illness. Make an appointment to see your family doctor, your child's doctor or a mental health professional. Write down how long the signs and symptoms last, how often they occur and give examples. This information will help a doctor or a therapist better understand your child's emotional state.

Source: Modified from Dubuque S.E.A., *Parent's Survival Guide to Childhood Depression* (King of Prussia, PA: Center for Applied Psychology, 1996).

how little they eat becomes an obsession. This often results in unusual eating habits, including eating small quantities of only a few foods. People with anorexia nervosa may also compulsively exercise, vomit, use laxatives, or take other medications to control their weight.

Bulimia nervosa involves uncontrolled eating and then purging the food to avoid weight gain. Bulimia nervosa is often associated with depression and tends to occur in families where one or more family members have been depressed.

**An anxiety disorder.** Some kids worry a lot. They fear what the future holds, fret about past experiences or worry that they can't handle the present. Anxiety problems vary greatly in severity. Some children are able to handle their anxiety and function quite well, but others have great difficulty doing so. Like adults, young people also may experience specific types of anxiety disorders such as obsessive-compulsive disorder or panic attacks. If your child has an anxiety disorder, he or she may:

- Be painfully self-conscious
- Need constant reassurance
- Seem tense and unable to relax
- Be overly concerned about his or her appearance

Physical signs may include:

- Nail biting
- Thumb sucking
- Hair pulling or twisting
- Difficulty falling asleep

Children who are anxious can appear to be overly mature. They strive to be perfect and can be extremely sensitive to criticism, frequently resulting in hurt feelings. They may have warm, caring relationships, but they're preoccupied with succeeding and being accepted and liked. Sometimes this anxiety comes from parents putting excessive pressure on their children to succeed.

**Substance abuse.** Unfortunately, in today's society almost all youth are exposed to alcohol and drugs at some point while they're growing up. Many experiment with these substances, and some develop disabling patterns of use. Though there's still a lot to learn about substance abuse in this age group, many factors may increase a child's vulnerability. However, the most critical risk factor for alcohol or drug abuse is a family history of chemical dependence.

In children and teenagers, many of the signs and symptoms of drug or alcohol abuse are similar to those of depression:

- Is vague, withdrawn or volatile
- Skips classes or has had a sudden drop in grades
- Makes secretive phone calls or arranges mysterious meetings
- Sleeps more or less than usual
- Has lost weight for no apparent reason

- Often borrows or steals money
- Doesn't get along with family and old friends as well as he or she used to
- Has made new friends and is fiercely loyal to them

**Post-traumatic stress disorder.** Children or teenagers who survive a horrific experience, such as a school shooting, a fire, a serious car accident, or sexual or physical abuse, may develop persistent emotional and behavioral problems because of their trauma. They may develop symptoms such as headache, stomachache or sleep problems. They also may react to trauma differently than do adults. They may:

- Be afraid of leaving their parents or fear losing them, and as a result not want to do anything new or unfamiliar
- Re-enact their experience through symbolic play or by actual behavior
- Act as they did at an earlier age when they were less mature

Young people with post-traumatic stress disorder often blame themselves and assume responsibility for what happened even though they couldn't have done anything to prevent the event. They may feel hopeless and pessimistic about the future, even years after the traumatic experience. Children and teenagers with pre-existing depression or an anxiety disorder or who have experienced an earlier loss are at the highest risk of developing post-traumatic stress disorder.

For more information on combined disorders, see Chapter 14.

## Treating depression in youth

The sooner depression is recognized and treated, the better. Even though children and teenagers have a high rate of recovery from a single episode of depression, they're at risk of subsequent episodes.

The most common treatments for children and teenagers experiencing depression are medication, psychotherapy or a combination of both. Opinions vary as to which form of treatment should be used first. Growing evidence shows that for most young people the best approach is a combination of medication and a form of psychotherapy called cognitive behavior therapy. A combined approach is especially important for severe depression.

## Medication

Until recently, doctors have been reluctant to prescribe antidepressants to children and teenagers because not much evidence has been available regarding the safety and effectiveness of these drugs in young people. However, recent studies indicate that some newer antidepressants, especially the selective serotonin reuptake inhibitors, are safe and effective. Additional research is needed to evaluate their long-term use in children and teenagers. Often antidepressants are combined with psychotherapy. Some studies suggest this two-pronged approach can be more effective than use of antidepressants alone.

Antidepressant medications are generally a first choice of treatment among doctors when a child or a teenager:

- Has severe symptoms that likely won't respond well to psychotherapy
- Doesn't have immediate access to psychotherapy
- Has psychosis or bipolar disorder
- Has chronic depression or recurring episodes

It's generally best to continue the medication for at least several months after symptoms of depression have subsided to help prevent a recurrence. When it's time to discontinue the drug, slowly taper off of the medication over a period of weeks or months with the help of your doctor. If depression recurs — especially while tapering off of the medication or shortly thereafter — it's usually necessary to resume the medication.

## Psychotherapy

Certain types of short-term psychotherapy, especially cognitive behavior therapy, have been shown to relieve symptoms of depression in children and teenagers. When a child or a teenager is depressed, he or she often has distorted, negative views, which reinforce the depression. Cognitive behavior therapy helps young people develop more positive views of themselves, the world and their life situation. Research suggests this type of therapy seems to

**Bipolar disorder in youth**

Bipolar disorder, also called manic-depressive disorder, occurs less commonly in teenagers than in adults, and rarely in children. It involves extreme swings in mood from euphoria (mania) to depression. Having a parent with bipolar disorder increases a teenager's or a child's risk of the illness.

As many as 20 percent to 40 percent of teenagers with major depression develop bipolar disorder within 5 years after the onset of depression. If bipolar disorder begins in childhood, it seems to be a more severe form of the illness than if it develops during teenage years or young adulthood.

If your child has the following symptoms, he or she should be evaluated by a psychiatrist or psychologist with experience in bipolar disorder, especially if you have a family history of the illness:

- Depression
- Abnormally high energy level combined with an inability to concentrate
- Excessive temper outbursts and mood changes

An accurate diagnosis is critical because medications often prescribed for other mental illnesses may worsen or trigger mania. This includes certain antidepressants. To prevent mania, an antidepressant needs to be combined with a mood stabilizer such as lithium (Eskalith) or valproic acid (Depakote).

The dilemma is how to effectively and safely treat bipolar disorder in children and teenagers. Right now their treatment is based on experience with adults. Although knowledge as to the effectiveness and safety of adult medications in children and teens remains limited, some good studies have been completed, and more research is underway.

be more effective than group or family therapy. It can also work faster than other forms of psychotherapy.

When working with children, mental health professionals typically modify the approaches they use for adults and teenagers. For instance, a therapist may use the child's drawings and storytelling to help him or her express feelings and problems.

Sometimes a therapist may recommend continuing psychotherapy for a period of time after the depressive symptoms are gone. This may further enhance a child or a teenager's coping skills, decreasing risk of a relapse. The therapist can also aid in early recognition and treatment should depression recur.

### Education

An important aspect of treating depression in young people is educating both the child and the parents about the illness and its treatment. Understandably, you may have many questions and concerns. Don't be afraid to ask questions of a family doctor or a mental health professional. The more you know and understand, the more likely the treatment will be successful.

## Greater emphasis on early intervention

In response to the growing rate of depression in children and teenagers, more efforts are being made to reduce depression in this age group. Studies suggest that early treatment of mild to moderate depression may help prevent severe depression and other related disorders, such as substance abuse and eating disorders.

Other studies show that among depressed young people, cognitive behavior therapy combined with relaxation training or group problem solving is helpful in preventing recurrences of depression for 9 to 24 months following treatment.

On another front, short-term family-based educational intervention seems to help reduce the risk of a first episode of depression or other mental illnesses in children and teens who are at high risk because of family history.

## Chapter 14

# *Combined disorders*

A s discussed in previous chapters, depression doesn't always occur by itself. It often accompanies other mental illnesses, most commonly anxiety, eating and personality disorders, and substance abuse.

With combined disorders, it can be difficult to sort out the relationship between the two. Did they develop independently of each other and now simply coexist? Are they reinforcing each other — each disorder making the other one worse? Did one disorder lead to the other? Which was present first?

When depression and another mental illness are combined, treatment can be more difficult. The first challenge in successfully treating combined disorders is recognizing the presence of both. For example, someone may have a long-standing unrecognized and untreated anxiety disorder now complicated by depression. The person may seek treatment for depression, but unless and until the anxiety disorder is recognized and effectively treated, there's a good chance the depression will persist or keep coming back. Or an individual experiencing depression may try to "medicate" himself or herself by drinking excessive alcohol, using illicit drugs or taking large amounts of prescription medications. If a doctor isn't aware of the substance abuse, he or she can't take it into account in treatment, and chances for a successful outcome are reduced. The only way to untangle the intricate interdependence of combined disorders is to recognize and treat both conditions.

## Anxiety and depression

Like depression, the term *anxiety* can mean different things. In common usage it refers to frequent and natural feelings you may experience from time to time when under stress. Meeting tight deadlines, driving in bad weather or rushing your kids from one place to the next can all cause you to feel anxious and tense. Anxiety can also be a symptom of or form of mental illness, a condition in which you may be anxious much of the time or easily become anxious when dealing with common situations.

Anxiety frequently occurs with depression. Up to 50 percent of depressed people experience anxiety. When their depression is treated, their anxiety often improves as well. The most effective treatment for combined anxiety and depression is a combination of medication and psychotherapy. Anxiety that isn't accompanied by depression usually is associated with an anxiety disorder:

**Generalized anxiety disorder.** Recurring or excess fears or worries best characterize generalized anxiety disorder. You find yourself stewing about something all of the time. You may be plagued by a sense of self-doubt and indecisiveness and have a nagging sense that something bad is about to happen. When you don't have anything to worry about, events in your life are generally positive.

**Social anxiety disorder.** People who are excessively fearful of social situations have social anxiety disorder, also called social phobia. You may become anxious when you're around people who you don't know, or you may fear a particular situation, such as talking in front of others. Other types of phobias include fears of flying, heights, certain animals and enclosed spaces.

**Obsessive-compulsive disorder.** People with obsessive-compulsive disorder have persistent, uncontrollable obsessions, compulsions or both. Obsessions are persistent, uncontrollable thoughts, such as repeated worries of making a mistake. Compulsions are uncontrollable behaviors. Classic examples include excessive hand washing or housecleaning to get rid of germs, or repeatedly checking to make sure a door is locked.

**Panic disorder.** Panic attacks that accompany panic disorder produce sudden, intense and unprovoked feelings of terror and dread, during which your heart may race, you may sweat and you may believe you're going to die. About half the people who experience panic attacks experience at least one episode of depression.

**Post-traumatic stress disorder.** People who've experienced a physical or emotional trauma, such as a natural disaster or a violent crime, may develop post-traumatic stress disorder (PTSD). You may experience memories of the event that seriously affect how you think, feel and behave. There's growing evidence that depression develops after prolonged PTSD, but depression can also precede the disorder.

## Substance abuse and depression

Studies indicate that more than half the people who abuse alcohol or drugs have another mental illness, or have experienced one in the past. About 20 percent of people who abuse drugs have major depression or have experienced it in the past. Of people who abuse alcohol, about 30 percent meet the medical criteria for depression.

The obvious question is, Why are these rates so high? Unfortunately, the answers aren't clear. Researchers do know that addictive substances, such as alcohol and drugs, act on many of the same brain neurotransmitters that influence mood. Some experts speculate that some people abusing alcohol or drugs may be trying to "normalize" their neurotransmitters in an attempt to feel better. But this effort is ill fated because even moderate amounts of alcohol or other substances can trigger or worsen depression.

Both substance abuse and depression must be addressed for your treatment to be successful. But that doesn't always happen. For example, you might enter a treatment program for drug abuse, but your depression may not be recognized and treated. Or a professional will treat your depression but not treat, or possibly not even recognize, your substance abuse problem.

Treatment for alcohol and drug abuse typically begins with supervised withdrawal from the substance and continued abstinence. Other aspects of treatment include professional support, education, psychotherapy and sometimes medications. Until you're in control of your substance abuse problem, treatment for depression has little chance of working. It's not uncommon for symptoms of depression to improve or resolve during treatment for substance abuse, without need for antidepressant medication.

## Eating disorders and depression

If you have an eating disorder, you may also be depressed. Fifty percent to 75 percent of people with anorexia or bulimia nervosa have a history of depression, and more than 50 percent of people with binge-eating disorder have symptoms of depression.

**Anorexia nervosa.** People with anorexia nervosa view themselves as fat even if they're underweight, and they go to great lengths to keep a low body weight. They eat very little and may compulsively exercise, to the point of starvation. Serious medical complications or death may result. Signs and symptoms of anorexia nervosa include:

- Resistance to maintaining a healthy body weight
- Irrational fear of gaining weight, even if underweight
- Unrealistic view of body shape and size
- Denial of the seriousness of a low body weight
- Among women, infrequent or absent menstrual periods

**Bulimia nervosa.** Bulimia nervosa involves eating large amounts of food within a short period (bingeing) and then purging the food through vomiting, enemas, laxatives or diuretics. People with this disorder may also exercise compulsively. Between bingeing and purging episodes, people with bulimia nervosa generally restrict how much they eat. Feelings of disgust and shame related to the illness can trigger further bulimic episodes, leading to the development of a vicious cycle. Excessive purging causes changes in body chemistry and may produce serious medical complications, or even death.

**Binge-eating disorder.** A binge-eating episode involves a loss of control over your eating behavior, resulting in the consumption of excessive amounts of food in a short period of time. The disorder isn't the same as an occasional episode of overeating when dining out or enjoying your favorite food. Binge-eating disorder is defined as having at least two days of binge-eating episodes a week over a 6-month period. Unlike bulimia nervosa, an eating binge isn't followed by purging of the food or excessive exercise. Weight gain, lowered self-esteem and other unhealthy effects from eating large amounts of food high in fat and high in sugar can result in serious medical complications.

Specific traits tend to be tied to various eating disorders. People with anorexia nervosa are more likely to be perfectionists, whereas people with bulimia nervosa are more likely to be impulsive. Binge eaters, as well as people with bulimia nervosa, tend to be preoccupied with weight and body image and, similar to people with anorexia nervosa, often have high personal standards. Teenage girls and young women account for about 90 percent of the cases of anorexia and bulimia nervosa. These eating disorders may also occur in older women and males, but only infrequently. Binge-eating disorder, on the other hand, is most common in adult, overweight women.

In general, eating disorders, like depression, often involve a complex interplay of medical, psychological and social factors. Studies indicate that the severity of your eating disorder may be closely tied to the severity of your depression, and they show that treating depression often helps alleviate anorexia or bulimia symptoms and reduces the frequency of binge-eating episodes. Antidepressants can be an effective treatment for bulimia nervosa even if you're not depressed. A recent study strongly suggests that bulimia nervosa may be linked to changes in the activity of the brain neurotransmitter serotonin.

At the very least, treating depression can help improve your mood and outlook so that you can concentrate on overcoming your eating disorder. It's important to treat eating disorders early, before the abusive pattern of eating becomes ingrained and more difficult to overcome.

## Body dysmorphic disorder and depression

Body dysmorphic disorder is characterized by a distressing preoccupation with a real or imagined flaw in your appearance. People with this disorder get so consumed by a distorted image of themselves that they have trouble functioning, and many even contemplate suicide. The disorder is often accompanied by depression.

Unfortunately, people with body dysmorphic disorder often conceal their preoccupation from others because they feel shame and embarrassment about their condition. Even though they may be getting treatment for depression, their disorder often goes undiagnosed. Until it's recognized and treated, efforts to treat only the depression are often unsuccessful.

Body dysmorphic disorder generally responds best to a combined treatment approach, including antidepressant medications. It may take longer to effectively treat combined depression and body dysmorphic disorder than depression alone. You may also require a higher dose of medication than what's generally prescribed for depression alone.

## Personality disorders and depression

Personality disorders most often develop by young adulthood. Individuals with personality disorders generally have a long-standing pattern of behavior that frequently involves trouble relating to other people. There are several types of personality disorders. Borderline personality disorder (BPD) and dependent personality disorder are the two personality disorders most commonly associated with depression.

**Borderline personality disorder.** People with BPD have a pattern of instability on many levels — in their relationships, their self-image and their mood. They often threaten and attempt self-injury or suicide. Some mutilate themselves by scratching or cutting on themselves or burning themselves with a hot object. In short, life for people with BPD can be described as a bumpy emotional roller coaster ride. Their behavior has been described as predictably unpredictable or characterized by stable instability. An individual with borderline personality disorder may:

- Have difficulty controlling emotions or impulses
- Experience frequent ups and downs
- Act impulsively
- Swing from one mood to another
- Have stormy relationships
- Become intensively angry and get involved in physical fights
- Think only in terms of black or white, good or bad
- Often feel empty inside
- Not want to be alone

Severe depression and anxiety frequently coexist with BPD. Psychotherapy — usually a variation of cognitive behavior therapy — is the bedrock of treatment for BPD. The therapy is designed to lessen or eliminate unhealthy behaviors and help people learn how to adapt better to life circumstances. Antidepressants, possibly combined with other psychiatric medications, may be prescribed when significant depression or anxiety accompanies BPD.

**Dependent personality disorder.** People with this disorder have a strong emotional need to be cared for, which typically results in passive, submissive and clinging behavior. Dependent personality disorder usually begins by early adulthood and includes many of these signs and symptoms:

- Feels an extreme need to be taken care of
- Feels incapable of getting along on his or her own
- Needs constant reassurance from others
- Has difficulty making decisions without considerable help from others
- Doesn't disagree with others for fear they'll disapprove
- Can't initiate projects or do things on his or her own
- Goes to great lengths to get care and support from others, even to the point of volunteering to do unpleasant tasks
- Feels helpless when alone
- Searches frantically for another person to turn to when a close relationship ends
- Is preoccupied with fears of having to care for himself or herself

## Telling it like it is

More research is needed to better understand the many complexities of combined disorders and how best to treat them. Although combined disorders are common, the intermingling and intensity of symptoms can present challenges and obstacles that require careful, accurate diagnosis. One way you can help yourself is to be honest and forthcoming when you discuss your symptoms with your health care provider. This can help him or her greatly in recognizing both conditions and determining the best treatment approach.

# Part 4

## Living With a Depressed Person

## Chapter 15

# Suicide and coping with suicide

More than 30,000 Americans commit suicide each year, and an estimated 10 to 20 times that many people attempt suicide. The suicide rate in this country is higher than the homicide rate. For every two people killed by homicide, three people die of suicide.

About 9 out of 10 people who commit suicide have one or more mental illnesses, most commonly depression. An often quoted statistic is that 15 percent of people with depression will commit suicide. However, a recent Mayo Clinic study suggests the actual rate may be lower. Researchers found the suicide rate for people receiving treatment for depression varies between 2 percent and 9 percent. People at the highest risk level were those recently hospitalized for attempted suicide. Those at the lowest risk level were individuals treated as outpatients. Other studies indicate people with untreated depression have a higher suicide rate than people receiving treatment. In short, the more severe the depression — especially if untreated or inadequately treated — the greater the suicide risk.

## Who's at risk?

It's impossible to predict with certainty who will kill themselves, or try. That's because suicide is a complex behavior. Many medical, psychological and social factors, such as depression, substance abuse, a personal crisis, and the availability of firearms or a lethal supply of drugs, can put a person at risk of suicide. Response to these risk factors varies dramatically from person to person.

To lessen the risk of suicide, it's important to be aware of key factors associated with its occurence. Your loved one may be at risk of suicide if he or she:

**Is depressed.** More than half the people who commit suicide have a form of depression, such as major depression or bipolar disorder.

**Has previously attempted suicide.** Between 20 percent and 50 percent of people who kill themselves have tried before.

**Is abusing alcohol or drugs.** Substance abuse can lead to unemployment, poor health and little or no emotional support — risk factors for depression. Alcohol and drugs can worsen depression by impairing judgment and causing people to act on impulse.

**Has a family history of suicide.** A study sponsored by the National Institute of Mental Health showed that one in four people who attempted suicide had a family member who did the same.

**Is male.** Women attempt suicide more often than men, but men are more likely to succeed. Of the more than 30,000 suicides committed in 1998, more than 24,000 were by men. Researchers can only speculate about why the suicide completion rate is higher among men. One possibility is that men generally use more lethal means, such as firearms, when attempting suicide. Women more often attempt suicide by overdosing on drugs or taking poison.

Among men, those at highest risk are white men older than age 85. Their suicide rate is six times higher than the national average. Interestingly, more than 70 percent of older men who kill themselves visited their doctor in the previous month, many with a depressive illness that wasn't detected. (Some 40 percent saw a doctor within the past week, and 20 percent that same day.) Most older men who commit suicide live alone. Often in frail health and with many of their loved ones no longer living, they may feel isolated, alone and helpless.

**Has access to a gun.** In the United States, most people who kill themselves do so with a gun. The availability of a firearm to a depressed person with suicidal thoughts increases the risk of suicide.

# Warning signs

Often several warning signs indicate that a loved one may be headed in the wrong direction and be at risk of suicide. Many of these warning signs are also features of depression, and it can be difficult to determine if the behavior may be a warning of suicidal intentions or simply a symptom of depression. That's why it's important to recognize possible depression and get appropriate help as soon as possible.

**Suicidal threats.** Sometimes an individual will tell others outright that he or she is thinking of committing suicide. Or the person might try a less direct approach, such as saying that everyone would be better off if he or she had never been born or was dead. The common assumption that people who threaten suicide don't commit suicide isn't true. Take their words as a sign of needing professional help.

**Withdrawing from others.** People at risk of suicide may be less willing to talk with others or may want to be left alone. Trouble at work or poor grades in school can be other signs of withdrawal.

**Moodiness.** We all have our ups and downs. But drastic mood swings — an emotional high on one day and deep discouragement the next — aren't normal.

**Personality changes.** Before someone commits suicide, often you may notice marked changes in his or her personality and routines, such as eating or sleeping patterns. For example, an individual who's often shy becomes the life of the party, or an outgoing individual becomes withdrawn.

**Risky behavior.** Uncharacteristically dangerous activities, such as high-speed driving, unsafe sex or drug abuse, may be a sign of an emerging desire to die.

**Personal crisis.** Major life setbacks, such as divorce, a lost job or the death of a loved one, can be difficult for anyone to manage. Among people who are depressed, a crisis like this can push them over the edge, triggering a suicide attempt.

**Giving away possessions.** Sometimes before committing suicide a depressed individual will give away his or her cherished possessions, believing that they won't be needed any longer.

**Beginning recovery.** Surprisingly, many people kill themselves 2 to 3 months into their recovery from depression. If your family member or friend has been struggling with depression for months or years, this may be the first time he or she sees the problems the depression has caused or the first time he or she has the emotional energy to act on a suicidal threat. Because your loved one may not yet have overcome the hopelessness and negative thinking that commonly accompany depression, these feelings combined with increased energy can lead to a suicide attempt.

## Dealing with suicidal thoughts and actions

Family and friends need to keep in mind that not everyone who thinks about suicide attempts it. But it's important to take any mention of suicide seriously, especially if you know or suspect that the person speaking of it is depressed. The best way to find out if a loved one is having suicidal thoughts or intentions is to ask. Don't worry that you'll plant the idea or push the person into something he or she had no intention of doing. What you will do is offer an opportunity to talk and, if your loved one is having suicidal thoughts, to discuss the pain and negativity fueling those thoughts. This can help decrease suicide risk. Keep in mind that your task is not to become the therapist but rather to convey your concern and get your loved one appropriate medical care, if needed. When you talk about suicide, be direct. Here are some questions to ask:
- Are you thinking about dying?
- Are you thinking about hurting yourself?
- How and when would you do it?

When discussing suicide, don't promise confidentiality, even if you think it's the only way to get the person to talk. To enlist professional help, you may have to share the information with others. If you promise not to tell and have to break your promise, then you'll betray the person's trust and possibly curtail your future ability to help.

In the face of possible suicide, be supportive, be empathetic and take whatever preventive actions are necessary. Remove or secure

## Involuntary hospitalization

Involuntary hospitalization isn't common, but it can occur. It's a legal procedure used when a person is at risk of harming himself or herself or others and refuses treatment. A person with severe depression might be involuntarily hospitalized for evaluation or treatment if he or she:

- Has made a suicide attempt
- Has persistent thoughts of suicide with a plan to carry out the act
- Is unable to provide basic needs for himself or herself, including not receiving adequate nutrition or taking appropriate health measures

In most states a person can be involuntarily hospitalized for psychiatric evaluation by a court order or by an order of a doctor for a limited time. If the evaluation finds cause for concern and the person still refuses treatment, a court hearing may be sought to determine if — in the eyes of the court — the individual is indeed mentally ill and in need of treatment. If the court determines this is the case, it may order involuntary commitment for mental health treatment. Without a court order, an individual may not be involuntarily hospitalized except on an emergency short-term basis.

To seek more information on involuntary commitment, contact your local social services agency or a local mental health center.

guns, knives and anything else you can think of that could be used in a suicide attempt. You may also want to monitor use of all medications. In the face of an imminent threat, do whatever is necessary, even if it means calling the police or getting the person professional help against his or her wishes.

## Suicide survivors: Those left behind

It's estimated that on average every suicide leaves at least six people deeply affected by the death. That amounts to nearly 200,000 people a year suffering one of the most painful forms of grief that exists. Family, friends and co-workers left in the aftermath of suicide are commonly referred to as suicide survivors.

When an individual commits suicide — or tries to — that person's family and close friends are often devastated and experience intense and persistent pain. Suicide survivors may suffer through repeated nightmares and flashbacks of the suicide scene, and they may avoid people and places that remind them of the suicide. Some survivors lose interest in activities they once enjoyed and grow emotionally numb — feeling incapable of caring. Beyond bereavement, suicide survivors may themselves become depressed or develop another mental illness due to severe stress.

### Common emotions

If you're a suicide survivor, you may have experienced one or more of the following reactions. These emotions usually subside with time, but the process can take weeks to months. The emotions may also recur from time to time, particularly during a special holiday, such as a birthday or an anniversary that reminds you of your loved one.

**Shock.** Shock is typically your first reaction, along with emotional numbness. You can't believe what has happened. It feels like you're watching someone else's nightmare.

**Confusion.** Only about one-third of the people who commit suicide leave notes. But even notes may provide only partial answers as to why your loved one felt the need to take his or her life. Realizing that you may never know the answer is part of the healing process.

**Grief.** You may cry often and easily. Tears are an honest expression of how you feel about losing someone you love.

**Despair.** Feelings of sadness and loss can erode your appetite, sleep, energy level and relationships. This can lead to depression.

**Anger.** You might become furious at a doctor, a family member, a friend or yourself for not seeing the suicide coming. You may feel angry toward your loved one who committed suicide for hurting so many people. Feeling and expressing this anger also is part of the healing process.

**Guilt.** The "if onlys" come back to haunt you. If only you had noticed the warning signs, contacted a doctor or insisted on your loved one getting help. In time you'll realize that it wasn't your fault.

## Seek help

It's fairly common for suicide survivors to develop a mental illness, especially depression. You may also experience intense reactions that are similar to post-traumatic stress disorder. This can produce terrifying nightmares, make you afraid of expressing tender emotions, and keep you away from people and places you once enjoyed because they remind you of your loved one.

If you're having trouble dealing with the loss, don't hesitate to seek help from your doctor or a mental health professional. Otherwise you may not improve, and other problems may develop. Counseling or psychotherapy can help you cope with the crisis you're facing. Support groups made up of other suicide survivors also can help you find your way through the maze of emotions and physical changes you may be experiencing. Counseling or support groups led by trained professionals are especially important if you don't have adequate support from family and friends.

Many suicide survivors refuse to seek help because they think it's a sign of weakness. But it's just the opposite. Seeking help when you need it is a sign of strength. It's a sign that you're taking charge of the problem because you want your life back.

## Learning to cope

You may never fully recover from the suicide of a loved one and may always feel the loss. With time and help from others, however, the pain of the loss will begin to diminish. To nurture the healing, consider these suggestions:

- On days when you're feeling blue or just need to get your feelings out, talk with a family member or a friend who's a good listener.
- Stay in touch with your family and friends. It's tempting to withdraw from those close to you, but you need to maintain your social connections. Friends and family can also help divert your attention to other things.

- On special occasions, such as birthdays and holidays that you celebrated with the person who committed suicide, let yourself grieve. Don't hold back your feelings. If it would help you to feel better, change some family traditions that you now find too painful.

Finally, remember this important fact: It's OK to begin laughing and enjoying life again. You don't have to prove that you loved the person by lingering with your grief. Your sorrow and tears are one way of honoring your loved one. Picking up and carrying on with your life is another.

## Chapter 16

# *The role of family and friends*

Depression affects not just those who have it, but also those who care about them — family, friends and co-workers. If someone you care about is depressed, then one of the most important things you can do for yourself and for that person is to learn all that you can about depression and its treatment. Whether the person who's depressed is a parent, a spouse, a companion, a child or a dear friend, your being informed will aid your desire and ability to help, alleviate some of your fears and uncertainties, and give you strategies for coping.

Going through an episode of depression with another individual can be a very difficult experience. It requires patience and courage on both your parts. Here are some things you can do to help smooth the way — for both of you.

## Being there

If you've never experienced a depressive episode yourself, then it's impossible to know how worthless, helpless and hopeless a person can feel in the midst of one. Broadcast journalist Mike Wallace, who had several bouts of depression, wrote in the foreword of the book *How You Can Survive When They're Depressed*, by Anne Sheffield: "It's difficult to make others understand how desperate a deep depression can make you feel, how lost, how cope-less, how grim. And no light at the end of the tunnel." But even if you don't know what it feels like to be depressed, you can offer empathy and compassion to someone who is. Simply being there for that person can make a difference in the course of his or her illness.

To be able to help, you must understand that depression is a serious illness that requires professional attention. Depression isn't the result of a character flaw. It's not laziness. It's not simply a case of the blues. And people who are depressed aren't faking it, and they can no more snap out of their depression than individuals with diabetes or arthritis can snap out of their illness.

### How to be supportive

Once you understand that depression isn't something your loved one has control over, it may be easier for you to offer support and care. Here are some ways you can help:

**Express your concern.** Acknowledge the depressed person's pain without implying that you know how he or she feels. Listen if he or she wants to talk, but don't try to draw the person out and don't ask intrusive questions. Being withdrawn and uncommunicative is often part of the illness. Don't take it personally.

**Ask how you can help.** Your loved one may not have specific suggestions of things that you can do, but he or she will know that you're willing to be supportive.

**Offer hope.** Remind the individual that depression is treatable, and that he or she will likely get better. If your loved one is undergoing treatment, gently remind him or her that it takes time for treatment to work.

**Give positive reinforcement.** Depressed people often feel worthless, and they dwell on their faults and shortcomings. Remind your loved one of his or her strengths and competencies and how much he or she means to you.

**Keep your sense of humor.** You're likely to feel frustrated and even angry at times. That's OK, but try not to vent in front of the person who's depressed and don't take your anger out on him or her. Use humor when possible to diffuse tension and to lighten the atmosphere, but don't make jokes at your loved one's expense.

**Encourage healthy behavior and activities.** Invite your loved one to join you in doing activities or visiting family or mutual friends. But don't push and don't expect too much too soon. Also gently remind the individual of the importance of exercise and a healthy diet.

## Dealing with resistance

Sometimes convincing someone who is depressed that he or she has an illness and needs professional help takes effort. Instead of asking, "Are you depressed?" or saying, "I think you're depressed," gently explain why you're concerned. Without being critical, describe the changes you've seen in his or her behavior and moods. Then ask if something is going on and why he or she seems down.

It may take you several attempts before you can convince your loved one to seek help, but continue to try. Offer to go along to the appointment. This not only shows your support but also enables you to share your observations with the doctor, which could help in the diagnosis. Another option is to call or meet with the doctor ahead of time and express your concerns.

During treatment you may have to help with the medication regimen by issuing reminders or, in some instances of severe depression, actually administering the doses as prescribed to make sure the medication is being taken correctly. If you see signs of improvement — and you could be the first to notice — share your observations to offer encouragement and hope. If you don't see signs of improvement after the treatment has had time to work, suggest that your loved one make another appointment with his or her doctor or therapist, or, perhaps, seek a second opinion.

## Bearing the burden

Many people may be concerned about an individual who's depressed, but for the one or two people who are the actual caregivers, depression can take an even larger toll. Caring for someone who's depressed may be one of the greatest challenges you'll ever face. People who are depressed may be withdrawn, unpleasant and not willing to communicate. They may view your actions and concerns as interference or as pointless.

In the foreward to *How You Can Survive When They're Depressed*, here's how Mike Wallace describes what Mary, his then-partner and now wife, experienced during his depression:

*I was distinctly unpleasant company for just about anyone who came near, but especially for Mary, who had to put up with my unrelieved glumness and short temper. ... And there is no way properly to describe the anguish that a depressive can put his family through. Gloom, doom, no love, no real communication, short temper, and leave-me-alone faultfinding. Why more marriages don't break up under those desolate circumstances is a puzzle, for you know deep down the damage you're doing to the ones you care about, the ones who have to live through it with you and suffer from the depression fallout, and yet you feel somehow incapable of doing anything to lighten the burden for them.*

Spouses and loved ones of a depressed person not only face care-taking responsibilities but also often take over tasks that the depressed person is unable to handle for the time being. For instance, if your spouse usually takes care of all of your financial matters, you may have to take over until he or she improves.

### Is the strain too much?

While caring for your loved one, you may feel as if your life has been put on hold. However, it's important that you also take care of yourself. The Alzheimer's Association offers these 10 signs of caregiver stress. Although they're directed at people caring for someone with Alzheimer's disease, they're equally appropriate for individuals caring for a loved one who's depressed.

**Denial.** You fail to accept the illness and its effect on your loved one, yourself and your family.

**Anger.** You find yourself angry with the person who's ill, at others who don't understand what you're going through, at the doctor for not fixing the problem or simply at the world in general.

**Social withdrawal.** You cut out activities that once brought you pleasure and isolate yourself from your friends.

**Anxiety.** You worry excessively about what will happen day by day and in the future.

**Depression.** The stress of caring for your loved one puts you at risk of becoming depressed.

**Exhaustion.** You feel too tired to drag yourself through yet another day.

**Sleeplessness.** At night you toss and worry, unable to sleep because of the myriad troublesome thoughts that keep going through your mind.

**Irritability.** You snap at others or feel like climbing the walls.

**Lack of concentration.** You have difficulty keeping your mind on what you're doing and performing everyday tasks.

**Health problems.** The stress begins to take its toll, physically and mentally.

## Taking care of yourself

How you handle the situation and care for yourself during this difficult period can make all the difference in your own health and your ability to cope with your loved one's depression. Attending to your own needs isn't being selfish. By caring for your own health, you'll be able to provide more care for your loved one. The following steps may help manage and relieve your stress:

**Enlist help.** You can't do it alone. When possible enlist the aid of family and friends to take over some of your responsibilities. If people offer to help, then don't hesitate to accept. If people don't offer, then ask them to help you with specific tasks.

**Accept your feelings.** You'll undoubtedly become frustrated at times, and you won't always be able to hide your emotions. It's OK to tell your loved one that you're frustrated. Remember, though, that there's a difference between saying, "I'm fed up with you," and saying, "I love you, but sometimes I need some time for myself." Expressing your feelings this way can also help ease your guilt about having such feelings. Like your loved one who is depressed, you also may experience feelings of loss and grief. These reactions are normal.

**Seek advice and support.** Talk to a trusted friend or a family member or seek advice and treatment from a professional. Sharing your feelings can be tremendously therapeutic. You might also join a support group to gain emotional support and helpful information and advice.

To find a support group that's right for you, contact your loved one's doctor, your local mental health association, your clergy or a local hospital. You can also contact the mental health organizations listed in the back of this book (see page 185).

**Reserve time for yourself.** When a family member is depressed, the focus of the entire family tends to shift to that person. Don't neglect your own needs. Eat right, exercise and get plenty of rest. Get out socially and do things you enjoy. Many of the self-help strategies discussed in Chapter 10 can benefit caregivers as well as individuals recovering from depression.

## A balancing act

Living with someone who's depressed isn't easy. The situation can become even more difficult if you have others to care for. Remind yourself that you're only one person and you can do only so much. Requesting help from others or taking time for yourself isn't a sign of weakness. If you're stressed out, tired or develop health problems, you'll be less able to help your loved one.

Finally, keep telling yourself that there is light at the end of the tunnel. With proper treatment, most people experiencing depression do recover. Better days may be on the horizon.

# Facing and overcoming depression: A personal story

David Plevak didn't choose an Air Force career as his father had done; instead he became a physician. But he brought a soldier's creed to the field of critical care medicine — duty, discipline and unceasing effort. For him, it was a calling that left no room for personal weakness.

So the idea that he could one day be laid flat by depression was not merely foreign, it was shameful. "I thought that people who had a mental disorder were not as strong," he says. "I tended to look down on them and feel they should be in better control of themselves."

### Great expectations

For years, nothing slowed down. During his boyhood Plevak's family traveled with the military, even living in Japan for a while. While he was in high school, the family settled in the Midwest. He majored in biology at Marquette University of Milwaukee, and then graduated from the Medical College of Wisconsin. For residency, the period of physician training after medical school, he selected not one but two fields — internal medicine and anesthesiology — at Mayo Clinic, Rochester, Minn.

From early on he had bouts of anxiety, flagging energy and sleeplessness, but he steeled himself to keep going. "I'm not the smartest person in the world, but I always was able to make up for my lack of intellectual gifts by studying hard and working hard," he says. "I did this in grade school, high school, college, medical school, residency."

The sense of duty was leavened by his conviction that he had been called by Providence to be a healer. "I had a genuine feeling and caring for patients, a deep-down knowing in my heart that this is what I should be doing in my life," he says.

## 'Two types of illness'

Mental illness didn't fit into Plevak's concept of disease. Indeed his medical training in the 1970s and 1980s reinforced his conviction that there were two types of illness: "organic" disorders that arose from disturbances in the body and "nonorganic" disorders of the mind that were matters of self-control and will.

After residency he sought advanced training, but not in internal medicine, where aches and pains often are influenced by state of mind. He was drawn to critical care medicine where it's easy to see tangible proof of life-threatening illness or injury. A tube threaded into an artery helps diagnose a failing heart. A chest X-ray confirms pneumonia.

"These were 'real' illnesses that I could get my hands around and make some definite intervention," Plevak says. "I liked the idea that people were really sick, and they were not pretending. There were not a lot of psychological or psychosomatic problems in that."

## Vigilance

But even as Plevak mastered new skills, he couldn't relax. He feared that he might harm a patient by forgetting a task, missing a diagnosis or prescribing the wrong drug. He also felt pressure to shine in front of his superiors, to show he had the right stuff to be not just a good clinician but someone with research and administrative potential.

The pressure didn't let up when he completed his training and became a staff physician at Mayo Clinic. He developed a routine. At

5:30 a.m. he would drive to the gym, where, he says, he would "work myself to physical exhaustion." He would then report for a full day's work. He administered anesthesia in the operating room or supervised the intensive care unit. He taught young resident physicians, did research and wrote up his findings for medical journals.

The work was exhilarating and he earned recognition. "You feel very excited and happy that you're at Mayo and that you're indeed a good doctor and that you are publishing medical research," he says. "Your residents are telling you that you're a good teacher. You're getting a lot of good feedback, which is very thrilling, becoming a member of national and international organizations. All of these things are very seductive."

## Growing toll

By this time Plevak had a wife and children, but his responsibilities at work absorbed much of his attention. "It was hard at times for me to be present for my family," he says. "It was difficult for me to turn work off, and I'd be thinking about it at home."

He tried to cope with the tension by compartmentalizing his home life. "Your personal life is something that you do when everything else is taken care of," he says. "You think, 'This is all the time I can spend for myself and my family.'" He became chronically tired. At times, low back pain would flare, forcing him to ease up on his activities. "I hated it because it would slow me down," he says. "I was going at full speed and didn't like to slow down."

One summer, back pain struck again while he was facing publication deadlines and organizing two medical conferences. This time medication and rest didn't help. Physical therapy failed. The ache evolved into the worst back pain he'd had, and he had to lie still. "The inactivity was so foreign," he says. "I lost the rush from doing vigorous exercise, and I lost the rush that I got from taking care of patients in critical situations, from teaching, all those things that I loved doing."

Without his daily routine, Plevak didn't know how to fill his days. "I was at home, on the couch and I couldn't move," he says. "I really didn't know how to act at home. I really didn't know where I fit in. I'd never spent that much time at home. I was always away somewhere doing something bigger and greater than being at home." He had always based his sense of worth on being productive. "I lost the sense of who I was," he said.

### Surprising diagnosis

Tests revealed that a bulging disk in Plevak's vertebral column was pressing on his spinal canal. Although most cases of back pain from a protruding disk resolve with rest, medication and physical therapy, he became convinced that an operation was the answer, and he consulted a neurosurgeon. But the surgeon sent him to a neurologist, a specialist in nonsurgical treatment of nerve disorders.

Plevak described his symptoms — back pain that radiated into both legs and burning feet. He expected the neurologist to call in another surgeon, but his symptoms didn't conform to a typical neurological pattern. Instead, the neurologist called in Plevak's wife. Plevak became annoyed when talk shifted to his mood, appetite and energy level — a search for the signs and symptoms of depression. A psychiatrist interviewed him. Plevak admitted that he had been irritable, fatigued, withdrawn, had difficulty eating, sleeping and concentrating. He was persuaded to enter the hospital for treatment of severe depression.

### Reassessment

Plevak was stunned to find himself a patient on a psychiatric ward. "Here was a guy who had tried to avoid caring for people with mental illness by going into acute care medicine," he says. "Now I was living with mental illness. Indeed I had a mental illness myself, and I had to deal with that."

He was given antidepressant medication and began psychotherapy. At first he identified more with members of the health care team on the psychiatric ward than with other patients. As time went on, his attitude changed. "I moved from being part of the health care worker group to being part of the patient group, hanging around with the patients, eating with the patients, talking with them about their frustration."

He struggled to accept his illness. "I would wake up every morning in the hospital and just cry," he says. "I couldn't believe what had happened to me. How could I have fallen so far? I looked at it as a real embarrassment and disappointment to myself."

Family and friends weren't so harsh. So many visitors came that staff had to impose limits. Their support helped him change his perception of himself. "I realized that they loved me not because of what I was able to do or accomplish, but just loved me because I was me," he says.

Plevak found respite in nonwork activities. "I didn't feel that I had to be accomplishing something every minute of the day." He began to see that even his religious beliefs had been dominated by the feeling that he had to produce. His best friend, a minister, helped change this view. "I realized that in my faith I didn't always need to be doing something for God to love me, but that God would love me even in this embarrassed condition," he says.

### A new approach

After 3 weeks Plevak's condition improved enough for him to be discharged on medication, but he wasn't ready to return to work. For several weeks he stayed at home, which he found overwhelming at first. "I was used to being home just to sleep and maybe a couple of hours here and there," he says. "Now I was home all the time, and I didn't know how to act."

He started with housework — washing and painting walls. He devoted more time to his four children, who at the time ranged in age from 5 to 20. "Now instead of having planned events, I felt comfortable just being with them, sharing life," he says.

His back pain resolved.

### Blurred line between physical and mental illness

Most mental illnesses arise from a combination of heredity, biology and environmental influences. For a vulnerable person, stressful circumstances can trigger changes in brain chemistry that can result in depression.

People with depression or other mental illnesses may be unaware of their mental state or may be unwilling to acknowledge it. Periods of anxiety, insomnia and low energy that Plevak had brushed off earlier in life may have been early, mild episodes of depression. "It was the back pain and the leg burning associated with the depression that prevented me from ignoring it this time," he says.

## Negotiating the demands of medicine

Plevak gradually resumed his job responsibilities. But, believing that overwork and exhaustion had contributed to his illness, he gave up some time-consuming projects and learned to say no.

What advice would he give his college-age daughter if she chose medicine or another field with a demanding training program? "The current medical education system tends to mold and form us into some kind of a uniform package," he says. "I would tell her to try to avoid this, to try to maintain her individuality and those things that are important to her. The only way she's going to be able to maintain that sense of self, that sense of individuality, will be to give herself plenty of time to meditate, to pray, to introspect, to spend time with loved ones. Unless you make that investment, you'll find yourself caught in the whirlwind of it all."

Plevak has recovered from his depression. He wrote an essay about his experience for *Mayo Clinic Proceedings*, a journal for medical professionals. "I was thankful that I was able to reenter life changed, and with a different, healthier outlook," he writes. "I wanted to share that with others. I also wanted to speak up for the emotionally and mentally disabled who are not able to achieve a full recovery from their illness. I wanted to say that these people are ill not by any fault of their own, and they deserve the same kind of care and respect that we offer to our other patients."

His commitment to medicine remains. He believes he has grown as a doctor, especially in his attitude toward people with mental illnesses. "I feel that they are me. Now when I see people who are mentally ill or I see that a patient has a history of mental illness, I feel a personal bond. I feel that we have shared something."

# Additional resources

Contact these organizations for more information about depression. Some groups offer free printed material or videotapes. Others have material or videos you can purchase.

### American Academy of Child and Adolescent Psychiatry

3615 Wisconsin Ave. N.W.
Washington, DC 20016-3007
202-966-7300
Fax: 202-966-2891
*www.aacap.org*

### American Foundation for Suicide Prevention

120 Wall St., 22nd Floor
New York, NY 10005
212-363-3500 or 888-333-2377 (888-333-AFSP)
Fax: 212-363-6237
*www.afsp.org*

### American Psychiatric Association

1400 K St. N.W.
Washington, DC 20005
888-357-7924
Fax: 202-682-6850
*www.psych.org*

### American Psychological Association

750 First St. N.E.
Washington, DC 20002-4242
202-336-5500
*www.apa.org*

### Center for Mental Health Services

5600 Fishers Lane, Room 17-99
Rockville, MD 20857
800-789-2647
*www.mentalhealth.org*

## Mayo Clinic Health Information
*www.MayoClinic.com*

## National Alliance for the Mentally Ill
Colonial Place 3
2107 Wilson Blvd., Suite 300
Arlington, VA 22201-3042
703-524-7600
Help line: 800-950-6264 (800-950-NAMI)
Fax: 703-524-9094
TDD: 703-516-7227
*www.nami.org*

## National Depressive and Manic-Depressive Association
730 N. Franklin St., Suite 501
Chicago, IL 60610-7204
312-642-0049 or 800-826-3632
Fax: 312-642-7243
*www.ndmda.org*

## National Institute of Mental Health
NIMH Public Inquiries
6001 Executive Blvd., Room 8184, MSC 9663
Bethesda, MD 20892-9663
301-443-4513
Fax: 301-443-4279
*www.nimh.nih.gov*

## National Mental Health Association
1021 Prince St.
Alexandria, VA 22314-2971
703-684-7722 or 800-969-6642 (800-969-NMHA)
Fax: 703-684-5968
TTY: 800-433-5959
*www.nmha.org*

## National Mental Health Awareness Campaign
*www.nostigma.org*

# Index

**A**

Acupuncture, 110
Acute *vs.* chronic depression, 55
Addiction and depression, 14
Addison's disease, 24
Additional resources, 185–186
Adjustment disorders, 51–52
Adrenal glands, 34, C1
Adrenal hormones, 33–34
Aging and depression, 139–144
    Alzheimer's disease, 26,
        141–142
    brain images, C8
    declining sex hormones, 35
    grief, 6–7, 19, 120–121, 140
    Parkinson's disease, 26, 142
    physical illness, 139
    recognizing depression,
        140–141
    retirement, 140
    stroke, 15, 25, 143
    treatment, 143–144
Alcohol abuse. *See*
    Substance abuse
Alcohol and depression, 41,
    140, 157
Alzheimer's disease, 26, 141–142
Anger management, 119–120
Anorexia nervosa, 29–30,
    148–149, 158
Anti-anxiety medications, 23,
    78–79

Anticonvulsants, 77–78
Antidepressant medications.
    *See also* Medications
    cost, 74–75
    dosage, 75
    duration, 76
    effectiveness, 73
    enzyme inhibitors (MAOIs),
        63, 72–73, C7
    mixed reuptake inhibitors, 70
    in pregnancy, 132
    receptor blockers, 71
    reuptake inhibitors and
        receptor blockers, 71–72
    selective serotonin reuptake
        inhibitors (SSRIs), 38,
        64, 69–70, C6
    serotonin reuptake inhibitors,
        69–70
    side effects, 73–74
    tricyclics, 63, 72
    in youth, 152
Antipsychotic medications, 79–80
Anxiety disorders, 28–29, 150
Anxiety and depression, 156–157
Atypical depression, 56, 147

**B**

Bad moods *vs.* depression, 6
Behavior changes and
    depression, 10
Binge-eating disorder, 30, 159

Bipolar disorders, 52–54, 153, C3
Body dysmorphic disorder
   (BDD), 30, 160
Borderline personality disorder
   (BPD), 30, 160–161
Brain imaging studies, 35–36,
   C2–C3
Bulimia nervosa, 30, 70,
   148–149, 158

**C**

Chemical dependence, 23.
   *See also* Substance abuse
Childhood abuse, 21–22, 36
Childhood depression, 145–154
   anxiety disorders, 150
   checklist for parents, 148–149
   eating disorders, 148–149
   post-traumatic stress
      disorder (PTSD), 151
   signs and symptoms, 146–147
   substance abuse, 150–151
   suicide risk, 145
   treatment, 151–154
Cognitive behavior therapy (CBT),
   63–64, 88–91, 152–154
Cognitive changes and
   depression, 9, 41
Combined disorders, 58, 155–162
Concentration. *See* Cognitive
   changes and depression
Coping skills
   active *vs.* passive style, 20
   anger management, 119–120
   for caregivers, 177–178
   for depressed older adults, 144
   for fighting depression, 111–112
   journaling, 121–122
   for suicide survivors, 171–172
   for women under stress, 137

corticotrophin-releasing
      factor blocker (CRF ), 81
Cortisol, 33–34
Counseling, 85–86
Cushing's disease, 24, 34
Cyclothymic disorder, 54

**D**

Demographics of depression, 3,
   7–9, 145
Dependent personality disorder,
   161
Depression
   age of onset, 7, 35, 50
   categories, 49–54
   in children, 145–154
   combined disorders, 155–162
   defined, 4–5
   diagnosing, 12, 39–48, 140–142
   history of treatments, 61–65
   incidence, 3, 7–9, 145
   in older adults, 139–144
   recurrence, 16, 50, 55
   risk factors, 17–30
   self-tests, 42, 46
   severity, 55–57
   suicide risk, 16
   symptoms, 9–10, 40–41,
      140–141, 146–147
   in teenagers, 145–154
   treatment, 67–110
   in women, 129–138
Dietary supplements, 81–84
Divorce and depression, 19
Domestic abuse, 136
Dopamine, 68, 80
Double depression, 51
Drug abuse. *See* Substance abuse
Drugs. *See* Medications
Dysthymia, 50–51

**E**

Eating disorders, 29–30, 158–159
Electroconvulsive therapy (ECT), 62–63, 97–105, 132, 144
Endorphins, 113
Estrogen and depression, 35
Euphoria, 52
Exercise
    and depression, 14–15, 113–114, 144
    getting started, 115
    health benefits, 114–115

**F**

Family and friends, 173–178
    being supportive, 174–175
    caregiving, 176–177
    discussing suicide, 168–169
    involuntary hospitalization, 169
    spotting suicide warning signs, 167–168
    survivors of suicide, 169–172
Family history, 17–18, 21, 23, 147, 166
Family therapists, 44
Family therapy, 93
Fatigue, 40, 147
Fish oil capsules, 83
5-HTP (5-hydroxytryptophan), 83–84
Food and drug interactions, 70, 73, 77, 82
Food and emotions, 116
Forgiveness, 120

**G**

Gender differences, 7, 30, 50, 129–130, 166
Generic medications, 74
Genetics, 18, 31–33

Getting help
    for loved ones, 151–152, 168–169, 175
    for yourself, 42–43
Grief, 6–7, 19, 120–121, 140
Group therapy, 92–93

**H**

Health care providers, 42–45
Healthy eating, 115–117
Heart disease, 15, 24
Herbal and dietary supplements, 70, 81–84
High blood pressure, 15–16
History of treatments, 61–65
Hormone replacement therapy (HRT), 135
Hormones and depression, 24, 33–35, C1
Hypothalamus, 34, 38, C1
Hypothyroidism, 24

**I**

Information resources, 185–186
Insight-oriented therapy, 93–94
Insomnia, 10, 14
Insurance concerns, 12–13, 88
Interpersonal therapy (IPT), 64, 91–92
Involuntary hospitalization, 169

**J**

Journaling, 121–122

**L**

Learned helplessness, 28
Life-changing events, 19, 51
Light therapy, 64, 105–107
Limbic system, 38
Lithium, 64, 77–78, 153

Loss and depression, 6–7, 19, 140, 171–172

**M**

Major depression, 49–50
Mania, 52–53
Manic-depressive disorder, 52–54
Medications. *See also*
    Antidepressant medications
  Accupril, 77
  Accutane (isotretinoin), 24
  Actron (ketoprofen), 77
  Advil (ibuprofen), 77
  Aleve (naproxen), 77
  alprazolam, 79
  amitriptyline, 72
  antipsychotic medications, 79–80
  Ativan (lorazepam), 79
  Aventyl (nortriptyline), 72
  Avonex (interferon), 23
  benzodiazepines, 23, 79
  bupropion, 70
  BuSpar (buspirone), 79
  buspirone, 79
  Carbatrol (carbamazepine), 77–78
  Celexa (citalopram), 69
  chlordiazepoxide, 23, 79
  citalopram, 69
  clonazepam, 79
  CRF (corticotrophin-releasing factor) blocker, 81
  Deltasone (prednisone), 23
  Depakote (valproic acid), 77–78, 153
  desipramine, 72
  Desyrel (trazodone), 71
  Dexedrine (dextroamphetamine), 75

Medications — cont.
  Dextrostat (dextroamphetamine), 75
  diazepam, 23, 79
  dosage, 75
  duration of treatment, 76
  Effexor (venlafaxine), 70
  Elavil (amitriptyline), 72
  Endep (amitriptyline), 72
  enzyme inhibitors (MAOIs), 63, 72–73, C7
  fluoxetine, 69
  fluvoxamine, 69
  gabapentin, 78
  Geodon (ziprasidone), 80
  Haldol (haloperidol), 80
  haloperidol, 80
  hydrochlorothiazide, 77
  HydroDiuril (hydrochlorothiazide), 77
  ibuprofen, 77
  imipramine, 63, 72
  Inderal (propranolol), 24
  interferon, 23
  iproniazid, 63
  isotretinoin, 24
  ketoprofen, 77
  Klonopin (clonazepam), 79
  Lamictal (lamotrigine), 78
  lamotrigine, 78
  Librium (chlordiazepoxide), 23, 79
  lithium, 64, 77–78, 153
  lorazepam, 79
  Lotensin, 77
  Ludiomil (maprotiline), 71
  Luvox (fluvoxamine), 69
  maprotiline, 71
  Mellaril (thioridazine), 80
  Methylin (methylphenidate), 75

Medications — cont.
methylphenidate, 75
Microzide (hydrochloro-
thiazide), 77
mirtazapine, 71
mood stabilizers, 77–78
Motrin (ibuprofen), 77
naproxen, 77
Nardil (phenelzine), 72
nefazodone, 71
Neurontin (gabapentin), 78
Nolvadex (tamoxifen), 24
nonsteroidal anti-inflammatory
drugs (NSAIDs), 77
Norpramin (desipramine), 72
nortriptyline, 72
Nuprin (ibuprofen), 77
olanzapine, 80
Orasone (prednisone), 23
Orudis (ketoprofen), 77
Pamelor (nortriptyline), 72
Parnate (tranylcypromine), 72
paroxetine, 69
Paxil (paroxetine), 69
phenelzine, 72
prednisone, 23
propranolol, 24
protriptyline, 72
Prozac (fluoxetine), 69
quetiapine, 80
Rebetron (interferon), 23
Remeron (mirtazapine), 71
risk factors for depression, 23-24
Risperdol (risperidone), 80
risperidone, 80
Ritalin (methylphenidate), 75
sedatives, 79
selective serotonin reuptake
inhibitors (SSRIs), 38, 64,
69–70, C6

Medications — cont.
Seroquel (quetiapine), 80
sertraline, 69
Serzone (nefazodone), 71
side effects, 73–74
Slo-phyllin (theophylline), 23
Stelazine (trifluoperazine), 80
substance P blocker, 80
Surmontil (trimipramine), 72
tamoxifen, 24
Tegretol (carbamazepine),
77–78
Theo-Dur (theophylline), 23
theophylline, 23
thioridazine, 80
Tofranil (imipramine), 63, 72
tranylcypromine, 72
trazodone, 71
tricyclics, 63, 72
trifluoperazine, 80
trimipramine, 72
Valium (diazepam), 23, 79
valproic acid, 77–78
Vasotec, 77
venlafaxine, 70
Vivactil (protriptyline), 72
Wellbutrin (bupropion), 70
Xanax (alprazolam), 79
ziprasidone, 80
Zoloft (sertraline), 69
Zyprexa (olanzapine), 80
Melancholia, 4, 56
Melatonin, 57, 106
Memory problems, 9, 141
Menopause, 35, 133, 135
Mental health professionals,
42–45, 88
Mood changes, 9, 41
Mood stabilizers, 77–78

**N**

Negative thinking, 89–90, 121
Nervous breakdown, 8, 54
Neurotransmitters, 37–38, 68,
    C4–C7
Norepinephrine, 37–38, 68

**O**

Obsessive-compulsive disorder
    (OCD), 29, 156–157
Obstructive sleep apnea, 26–27
Omega-3 fatty acids, 83
Optimists *vs.* pessimists, 27–28
Osteoporosis, 135
Outlook and depression, 20,
    27–28, 88–91, 121

**P**

Panic disorder, 29, 157
Parenting and depression,
    13–14, 146–147
Parkinson's disease, 26, 142
Pastoral counselors, 45
Perimenopause, 135
Personal care and depression, 40
Personal stories, 10–12, 102, 104,
    118, 134, 179–184
Pessimistic outlook, 27–28
Phototherapy (light therapy), 64,
    105–107
Physical symptoms of
    depression, 10, 40-41
Pituitary gland, 34, C1
Positive coping style, 20
Positron emission tomography
    (PET), 35
Postpartum depression, 56–57,
    132–133
Post-traumatic stress disorder
    (PTSD), 22, 151, 157

Pregnancy, 131–132
Premenstrual dysphoric disorder
    (PMDD), 130–131
Prevalence, 3, 7–9, 145
Psychiatric nurses, 44
Psychiatrists, 43
Psychoanalysis, 62
Psychodynamic therapy, 93–94
Psychologists, 43–44
Psychotherapy
    cognitive behavior therapy,
        63–64, 88–91
    *vs.* counseling, 86
    couples and family therapy, 93
    duration, 93–94
    group therapy, 92–93
    how it works, 94–95
    interpersonal therapy, 64, 91–92
    in older adults, 144
    selecting a therapist, 88
    in youth, 152–154

**Q**

Questionnaires, 47, 148-149

**R**

Rape, 136
Receptor blockers, 71
Recurrence of depression, 16, 50, 55
Relationships
    abuse, 28
    couples and family therapy, 93
    divorce or separation and
        depression, 19
    impact of depression, 13–14
    interpersonal therapy, 91–92
    learned helplessness, 28
Resources, 185–186
Retirement, 140
Risk factors, 17–30, 147

**S**

Sad moods *vs.* depression, 6
SAM-e (S-adenosylmethionine), 82
Seasonal affective disorder (SAD), 57, 105–107
Secondary depression, 57
Sedatives, 79
Self-help strategies, 111–126, 144
Self-tests for depression, 42, 46
Serotonin, 38, 68
Serotonin syndrome, 70, 82
Sex hormones, 34–35, 130–135
Sexual abuse, 21–22, 136
Shock therapy. *See* Electro-convulsive therapy (ECT)
Sleep problems
    apnea, 26–27
    excessive sleeping, 40
    insomnia, 10, 14
    self-help suggestions, 117–118
Snoring, 26–27
Social anxiety disorder, 29, 156
Social ties, 124–125
Social workers, 44
Spirituality, 125–126
St. John's wort, 70, 82
Stimulants, 75
Stress, 18–20, 122, 137
Stress hormones, 34
Stroke, 15, 25, 143
Substance abuse and depression, 14, 23, 150–151, 157–158, 166
Substance P blocker, 80
Suicide
    involuntary hospitalization, 169
    risk of, 16, 165–166
    survivors, 169–172
    thoughts of, 41, 168–169
    warning signs, 167–168
    in youth, 145

Support groups
    pros and cons, 124
    for suicide survivors, 171
Supportive therapy, 93–94
Symptoms, 9–10, 40–41, 140–141, 146–147

**T**

Talk therapy, 85
Tamoxifen and depression, 24
Teenage depression, 145–154
    anxiety disorders, 150
    bipolar disorders, 153
    checklist for parents, 148–149
    eating disorders, 148–149
    post-traumatic stress disorder (PTSD), 151
    signs and symptoms, 146–147
    substance abuse, 150–151
    suicide risk, 145
    treatment, 151–154
Testosterone and depression, 35
Thyroid disease, 24, 33
Thyroid glands, 33, C1
Transcranial magnetic stimulation (TMS), 108–109
Traumatic experiences, 20–21, 51
Treatment
    counseling, 85–86
    electroconvulsive therapy, 62–63, 97–105
    history of, 61–65
    light therapy, 64, 105–107
    medications, 67–81
    in older adults, 143–144
    outcomes, 13–16, 137
    psychotherapy, 85–96
    self-help strategies, 111–126
    transcranial magnetic stimulation (TMS), 108–109

Treatment — cont.
    vagal nerve stimulation
        (VNS), 109
    in youth, 151–154

**V**

Vagal nerve stimulation (VNS), 109

**W**

Web resources, 42, 185–186
Weight problems, 14, 30
Women and depression, 129–138
    body dysmorphic disorder
        (BDD), 30, 160
    borderline personality disorder
        (BPD), 30, 160–161
    childhood sexual abuse, 21–22
    coping skills, 137
    domestic abuse, 136
    eating disorders, 29–30
    estrogen levels, 35
    incidence, *vs.* men, 7
    menopause, 35, 133, 135
    oral contraceptives, 24
    postpartum depression,
        56–57, 132–133
    pregnancy, 131–132
    rape, 136
    seasonal affective disorder
        (SAD), 57, 105–107
    social and cultural issues,
        135–136
    tamoxifen, 24
    working mothers, 20, 136
Workplace problems, 14, 20

**Y**

Youth and depression, 145–154

# MAYO CLINIC ON HEALTH

Arthritis

Chronic Pain

Depression

Digestive Health

Healthy Aging

Healthy Weight

High Blood Pressure

Managing Diabetes

Prostate Health

Vision